What Went Wrong?

What Went Wrong?

Russia's Lost Opportunity and the Path to Ukraine

by
PHILIP YANCEY
and
JOHN A. BERNBAUM

CASCADE *Books* · Eugene, Oregon

WHAT WENT WRONG?
Russia's Lost Opportunity and the Path to Ukraine

Cascade Books
An Imprint of Wipf and Stock Publishers
199 W. 8th Ave., Suite 3
Eugene, OR 97401

www.wipfandstock.com

PAPERBACK ISBN: 978-1-6667-4797-3
HARDCOVER ISBN: 978-1-6667-4798-0
EBOOK ISBN: 978-1-6667-4799-7

Cataloguing-in-Publication data:

Names: Yancey, Philip, author. | Bernbaum, John A., author.

Title: What went wrong? : Russia's lost opportunity and the path to Ukraine / Philip Yancey and John A. Bernbaum.

Description: Eugene, OR: Cascade Books, 2024.

Identifiers: ISBN 978-1-6667-4797-3 (paperback) | ISBN 978-1-6667-4798-0 (hardcover) | ISBN 978-1-6667-4799-7 (ebook)

Subjects: LCSH: Yancey, Philip—Travel—Russia and Ukraine. | Evangelistic work—Russia. | Ukraine—History—Russian Invasion, 2022–.

Classification: DK288 W45 2024 (paperback) | DK288 (ebook)

VERSION NUMBER 013024

Contents

Preface | vii

Part One: The Cold War Thaws
Chapter 1: A Gust of Hope | 3

Part Two: Visit to a Shattered Empire
Chapter 2: Invitation to a Revolution | 11
Chapter 3: Rumblings from a Volcano | 15
Chapter 4: Church Bells in the Kremlin | 19
Chapter 5: Praying with the KGB | 25
Chapter 6: Basil and the Journalists | 32
Chapter 7: Interlude in Zagorsk | 39
Chapter 8: Man of the Decade | 48
Chapter 9: Fall from Grace | 54
Chapter 10: The Last Marxist in Moscow | 60
Chapter 11: Awakenings | 66

Part Three: Russia's U-Turn and Ukraine's Rebirth
Chapter 12: The Light That Dimmed | 77
Chapter 13: After the Fall | 80
Chapter 14: Putin's Ascent | 86
Chapter 15: Church and State | 92
Chapter 16: A Painful Past | 99
Chapter 17: Invasion | 105
Chapter 18: Dirty War | 113
Chapter 19: Holy War | 121

Part Four: Lessons Learned

Chapter 20: Culture Counts | 131

Chapter 21: "Who Are We?" | 138

Chapter 22: The Threat of Autocracy | 144

Chapter 23: Baptizing Caesar | 153

Chapter 24: What Went Right with Ukraine? | 159

Afterword: The Future for Ukraine and Russia | 165

Appendix: Project Christian Bridge | 171

Subject Index | 175

Preface

by John A. Bernbaum

IF YOU WERE BORN after 1989, you missed one of the most dramatic periods in world history. Some historians have described the time, when the Berlin Wall came crashing down and communism collapsed throughout Central and Eastern Europe, as the most pivotal era since the Reformation.

No one had predicted the quick, stunning disintegration of the Soviet Union as a superpower. Former United Nations ambassador Jeane Kirkpatrick commented, "Nothing like this has ever happened before—not in the history of empires, not in the modern period, certainly not among communist states."

Those of us who were old enough, and reasonably alert to world developments, witnessed a breathtaking sequence of events. It took the Poles ten years of strikes and protests to bring down the communist system in their country. The pace of change accelerated to ten months for the people in Czechoslovakia, ten weeks for the East Germans, and only ten days for the Romanians.

In the midst of this dramatic period, Philip Yancey and I were invited with seventeen other Christians to visit Moscow. Mikhail Gorbachev and Boris Yeltsin were asking us to help restore morality to the Soviet Union. As a journalist, Philip recorded our meetings with the leaders of Soviet communism, most of whom we found dazed and bewildered. Although schooled in Marxist ideology, very few still believed in its promises. Quite simply, they didn't know what to believe, hence their appeal for help.

This firsthand account needs to be preserved because it captures a truly remarkable event, one unique in history. I have never encountered a report of government leaders admitting to their rival powers the failure of Marxism-Leninism and discussing how religion is needed to hold their society together. It was an amazing time and the story should be retold.

After our visit, I moved to Moscow to establish the first Christian liberal arts university in Russia. The doors of freedom swung wide open, and investors, economists, and missionaries of all kinds poured into the country. It seemed that the Cold War had thawed, and Russia was joining the company of modern liberal democracies.

As we now know—and as I witnessed in person—after a tumultuous decade Russia took a different path, a slow U-turn away from the reforms of the 1990s. Vladimir Putin brought stability to the country and restored national pride, but at a cost: the cost of freedom for Russian citizens and then a much more devastating cost for the people of Ukraine.

At this critical moment in world history, Philip Yancey is reprinting the book he wrote in 1991, *Praying with the KGB*, as chapters 2–11 of this volume. He has asked me to set that book in historical context, with an introductory chapter giving background for our visit. In addition, we have collaborated on a follow-up account describing what happened afterward.

If you were too young to witness the former Soviet empire breaking apart, the events of 1991 described in these pages will likely surprise you. Most people have no idea that Soviet communists invited Christian leaders from the United States to help restore moral and ethical values to its imploding society. History is still unfolding, but one question remains: What went wrong? Why did the largest country in the world choose instead a different path?

PART ONE
The Cold War Thaws

by John A. Bernbaum

CHAPTER 1

A Gust of Hope

A GLOBAL RIVALRY THAT for decades threatened the entire planet traces back to World War II, the costliest war in human history and one that left at least seventy million people dead. The United States and the Soviet Union had been reluctant allies in the war against Hitler's Germany. Once victorious, these two countries became competitive superpowers on the world stage.

British writer George Orwell coined the term Cold War, to describe antagonists in conflict but stopping short of direct military confrontation. Both the US and the Soviet Union stockpiled tens of thousands of nuclear weapons, and for forty-five years Cold War tensions dominated world politics. The United States led NATO and the Western Bloc, referred to as the First World, while the Soviet Union led the Warsaw Pact and the Eastern Bloc, known as the Second World. (Many of the remaining, nonaligned countries—labeled the Third World—became battlefields in which the superpowers intervened, often militarily.)

Following the death of Joseph Stalin in 1953, Nikita Khrushchev and, later, Leonid Brezhnev became General Secretaries of the Communist Party—Khrushchev for nine years and Brezhnev for eighteen years. Brezhnev's lengthy term was often called the "era of stagnation." For observers in the West, Brezhnev's failing health and addiction to painkillers seemed to diminish the Soviet threat. His geriatric successors, Yuri Andropov and Konstantin Chernenko, each lasted only one year.

In 1983 the Center for Strategic and International Studies, one of Washington's leading think tanks, published a book titled *After Brezhnev*. The book revealed the findings of thirty-five scholars who had researched all the available intelligence on the Soviet Union and its outlook. These scholars concluded, "All of us agree that there is no likelihood whatsoever that the Soviet Union will become a political democracy or that it will collapse in the foreseeable future."

When the USSR went through three leadership changes in as many years, their conclusion seemed to be confirmed. But in 1985 Mikhail Gorbachev was chosen as general secretary of the Communist Party. The fifty-four-year-old Gorbachev represented a new generation; in fact, he was the first general secretary born after the 1917 Russian Revolution.

While in his thirties, Gorbachev had traveled to Belgium, the Netherlands, Germany, France, and Italy, an experience that profoundly affected him. His book *Memoirs* records that one question haunted him: "Why was the standard of living in our country lower than in other developed countries?" When he rose to the post of general secretary, he knew his mandate: to revive the Soviet economy and to institute reforms to elevate the standard of living for the Russian people.

One month after his selection, Gorbachev announced a new era of change, which we now know was only vaguely forming in his mind. Yes, the Soviet economy had stalled and badly needed modern technologies from the West. Yet he also believed that his nation suffered from a moral and spiritual malaise, an insight that many observers in the West overlooked.

Gorbachev introduced two Russian words into the global vocabulary. The first, *perestroika* or "restructuring," expressed the need for dramatic changes in Soviet economic and political systems. He sought to make fundamental reforms within the communist system without destroying it completely.

No leader of any country had successfully changed a Marxist-style command economy into a free market economy, so there were no precedents for Gorbachev to follow. Somehow he had to strike a balance between powerful traditionalists, who could block his reforms, and the beleaguered Soviet people, who might insist on even more radical changes. During his first year in power, he replaced a third of the country's top Communist Party officials. Next, Gorbachev scheduled the first free elections held in the Soviet Union since 1917, leading to his election as the Soviet Union's first president.

Glasnost (openness) was the second Russian word made famous by Gorbachev. He granted Soviets freedom of speech and assembly, something previously unknown in the USSR. Thousands of political prisoners were released and books previously forbidden now became available. Russians soon learned that they had indeed achieved equality with their fellow citizens, an "equality of poverty" encompassing more than 85 percent of the population. Journals and daily newspapers reported on the dark side of life under communism, such as the KGB's record of arrests and assassinations, and the government's history of destroying churches, mosques, and synagogues.

Another change received less attention in the West: Gorbachev's resolve to end the harsh persecution of Christians and other religious communities. He promoted the thousand-year anniversary of Christianity in Russia in 1988, and spoke about the importance of religious and moral values for the life of his country. This historic move severed the link between Marxism-Leninism and atheism, and ultimately Soviet legislators passed one of the most expansive laws on religious freedom in the world.

Gorbachev had more surprises: he also made a major shift in the Soviet Union's foreign policies. In order to focus all of his energies on reform at home, he began a unilateral withdrawal from the Cold War. He determined to lower tensions with foreign opponents, especially the United States. Unlike previous Soviet leaders, he harbored no cultural hostility toward the West, admired Westerners, and counted some of them as friends. He boldly set out to develop personal relationships with American presidents, meeting with President Ronald Reagan five times and President George H. W. Bush seven times.

World leaders, weary of the Cold War, began to propose major reductions in nuclear weapons and conventional forces. Gorbachev shocked the world in 1988 by announcing the full withdrawal of Soviet forces from Afghanistan after its painful ten-year struggle. Later that year, he repudiated the "Brezhnev Doctrine," which justified Soviet domination of Eastern Europe. His new approach allowed countries belonging to the Soviet alliance to act more independently and set their own domestic policies. Western correspondents dubbed this new policy the Sinatra Doctrine ("I did it my way").

Gorbachev continued to surprise by repudiating the Communist Party's claim to a monopoly on power. When he amended the constitution to remove the Communist Party as the only legal political party, more than four million Russians turned in their membership cards or stopped paying party dues.

It seemed that the Cold War had finally thawed. Gorbachev and his foreign minister, Eduard Shevardnadze, coined a new word to describe the relationship they sought with the United States: partnership (*partnerstvo*, a term adapted from English). They envisioned working together with the United States to solve some of the world's problems, a dramatic relaxation of the tension between superpowers that had prevailed for nearly half a century.

֍

As Gorbachev was combating resistance from hard-liners, a new star arose in the person of Boris Yeltsin, whom Gorbachev had appointed as the new leader of Moscow's Communist Party. Yeltsin quickly established himself as a populist leader, one who identified with the forces of democratic change. He turned down a spacious home as one of his prerogatives and chose to ride buses or trams to his office rather than chauffeured limousines. He attacked government leaders as being too complacent, not adequately supporting the common people during chaotic times.

Yeltsin shrewdly resigned from the Party's Politburo in 1987—the first person ever to do so—and three years later resigned from the Communist Party. Positioning himself as an advocate of reform and Russian nationalism, he was elected the first president of the Russian Republic in July 1991. Gorbachev remained president of the increasingly restive USSR.

In August 1991, Gorbachev's opponents staged a coup, putting all the reforms of the previous years in jeopardy. Gorbachev was placed under house arrest at his Black Sea resort while Soviet military forces rolled into Moscow, surrounding the Russian White House. Barricades went up to defend the government, and Muscovites rallied to take a stand against the coup. Yeltsin seized this opportunity by climbing on top of a tank in front of the White House and calling on the people to defend their newly created democracy.

For those of us in Moscow at that time, the coup was both frightening and exciting. We witnessed a forceful siege of the White House and then the collapse of the coup a mere three days later. I was meeting at a retreat center with a group of economics and business professors from the Christian College Coalition and their Russian colleagues. We spent those tumultuous few days glued to the radio and television. When the coup failed, we gathered in the courtyard at the retreat center, held hands, and, led by our new Russian friends, sang "We Shall Overcome" in English. We all felt a gust of hope for the future of the country.

When Gorbachev returned to Moscow, his power base began to break apart as supporters transferred their allegiance to Yeltsin. For a time, it was very difficult to know who was in charge, whether in Moscow or in the rest of the country. For supporters of democracy in Russia, the very atmosphere was charged with hope and freedom. Soviet society itself, however, was entering a transition period of confusion and chaos. The Russian population desired change, yes, but not revolutionary upheaval.

❧

Philip Yancey's account of our 1991 visit to Russia, *Praying with the KGB*, was subtitled *A Startling Report from a Shattered Empire*. Startling, indeed: for Westerners, the possibility of the USSR voluntarily moving toward democratic reform, after decades of autocratic rule, almost defied belief. People of faith especially, aware of the severe persecution of religion in the Soviet Union, now saw a new openness that would have been inconceivable just a few years before.

At the same time, life in the USSR was growing increasingly difficult: the ruble fell in value daily, food lines stretched on and on, and an anxious nation feared what might lay ahead. Such was the unsettled atmosphere when nineteen of us received a letter inviting us to come to Moscow at the behest of President Gorbachev, President Yeltsin, and leaders of other Soviet republics.

As you will learn when you read this book, the opportunity was unparalleled. I had made three previous trips to Russia, but never in my wildest dreams would I have imagined a chance to meet Gorbachev, the world-famous statesman, and Yeltsin, the people's champion who had confronted coup leaders from atop an army tank. Even now I can hardly believe what we encountered in Moscow during this sliver of time. Former communists freely confessed the failures of Marxism-Leninism and desperately yearned for Christian morals and ethics, which they now admitted were needed to save Russia from complete disintegration.

Despite the upheaval in Moscow and across the USSR, our delegation of nineteen felt that we were participating in a time of hope and renewal. American experts had insisted in 1983 that "there is no likelihood whatsoever that the Soviet Union will become a political democracy or that it will collapse in the foreseeable future." As we flew to Moscow in October of 1991, both of these outcomes seemed possible. Our invitation asked us to help restore morality to the Soviet Union—a tall order for an ad hoc delegation of American Christians.

PART TWO

Visit to a Shattered Empire

by Philip Yancey

*Of all that was done in the past, you eat the fruit, either rotten or ripe
. . . For every ill deed in the past we suffer the consequence.*

—T. S. ELIOT

CHAPTER 2

Invitation to a Revolution

A MEMORY FROM CHILDHOOD: An eye injury has kept me home from school, and all day I must lie still on the couch, with dark patches covering both eyes. My mother is ironing, and the hot, sour smell of pressed cotton fills the room. The radio, perpetually tuned to a Christian station, sends out a stream of string-heavy hymn arrangements until noon, when a gruff, familiar voice comes on. "Friends, it's Carl McIntire. Have you heard that Khrushchev claims to want peace? Sure, Khrushchev wants peace. A piece of this, a piece of that, until he has it all."

I grew up nourished on fear in a hotbed of southern conservatism. An uncle, warning of communist infiltration, packed up his family and moved to Australia. When the newspaper ran a photo of Khrushchev pounding his shoe on the table with the chilling caption, "We will bury you!" I took the threat literally. I practiced crawling under my school desk with my hands over my head, in the position we were to assume if Russia ever launched the Cuba-based missiles aimed our way. For the school science fair, I debated which model bomb shelter to build.

In the tenth grade, using money from my paper route, I purchased one hundred copies of a scary book called *None Dare Call It Treason*, which

I then distributed free to my classmates, like gospel tracts. Church further fed the fear. There I heard of Russian Christians condemned to slave labor in Siberian salt mines, and of martyrs in China who declared their faith just before the communists chopped off their heads. "What will you say when the communists take over here?" the pastor challenged us. "Will you confess Christ as Lord even if it means prison or death? Or will you deny him and compromise?"

I read somewhere that the communists examined the hands of their conquered foes for calluses. Uncalloused bourgeoisie they lined up and shot; those with worker hands they set free. I raked leaves with a passion, scorning gloves in order to coax the resulting blisters into calluses. I also read that communists spared anyone who spoke their language. My brother signed up for Russian classes and I studied Chinese, in hopes that one family member would survive an enemy assault from either direction.

Over the years, my politics mellowed and my fear subsided. Even so, nagging doubts remained—do any of us shake off the strangling fears of childhood? Every few years, until recently, *Time* magazine printed a map showing the global advance of world communism and each time, it seemed, the page got redder and redder. And just when I thought I had overcome my childhood hysteria, I read all three volumes, 1,877 pages, of *The Gulag Archipelago* by Aleksandr Solzhenitsyn. Was Carl McIntire right after all?

It was against this background that I received an invitation to travel to Moscow as part of a group called Project Christian Bridge. The letter, signed by the chairman and four other members of the Supreme Soviet, could, except for the flawed grammar and misquoted Bible reference, have been written by an American evangelist.

> In the difficult, often agonizing transitional period that our country is experiencing . . . spiritual and moral values acquire a great, if not paramount significance in their ability to guarantee us against confrontation, civil conflicts, the erosion of moral foundations, and the lowering of standards. . . .
>
> We know the role which your Christian organizations are playing as you following the great words of Christ: "Faith without works is dead." You are able to assist in the social development of a country and you are able to establish friendly relations with other countries, including the Soviet Union.
>
> All of this has caused us to address you with words of brotherhood and cooperation. We are certain that Soviet people, like American people, share a common striving for the ideas of

humanism, cleansing from filth, the celebration of good, love, and charity between our people and between all people of the world. We are charging the prominent Christian activist Mikhail Morgulis to act as our envoy and mediator in carrying our feelings and thoughts about cooperation and mutual assistance to Christian organizations in America.

[We wish to] implement moral ideas, to develop charitable funds and civil societies. We are prepared to assist in the meeting of leaders of Christian movements in the USA with deputies and the leadership of the Supreme Soviet of the USSR, President M. S. Gorbachev, President B. N. Yeltsin, and the leaders of other Soviet republics, whose people are devoted to the moral values of Christianity.

What's the catch? I wondered. Why were Communist Party leaders presenting themselves as concerned about filth, good, love, charity, and "moral foundations"? What did these people truly want from us?

More out of curiosity than anything else, I agreed on short notice to join the ad hoc delegation that included television and radio broadcasters, educators, lawyers, publishers, Russia specialists, pastors, businessmen, and mission executives. The Soviet government had promised to approve visas overnight and to pick up expenses within the country. It seemed an ideal way to visit Russia, bypassing the red tape that entangles many visitors.

Our delegation rendezvoused in the Frankfurt, Germany, airport in late October 1991. None of us knew what to expect from the trip. Changes were happening at lightning speed in the Soviet Union, making even the immediate future impossible to predict. For example, we had been promised a meeting with Gorbachev, but would he still hold an office by the time we got there? Would the Supreme Soviet, the nation's parliament, and our official hosts, even survive in view of independence demands by fractious republics?

When I returned on November 7, the seventy-fourth anniversary of the Bolshevik takeover, I no longer wondered why the Soviet government invited a delegation of evangelical Christians. A revolution had taken place in the great, sprawling land that spans eleven time zones, a revolution every bit as sweeping and monumental as the Bolshevik revolution that few Soviets deigned to commemorate on November 7.

"All history, once you strip the rind off the kernel, is really spiritual," said the British historian Arnold J. Toynbee. The recent events in the former Soviet Union demonstrate the truth of his statement. While Western media tend to focus on the economic crisis, wherever we went government officials and private citizens alike affirmed that the true crisis in their nation was moral and spiritual. We heard that opinion expressed so adamantly and so frequently that I came to see it as the great untold story of the USSR—and the reason behind the Soviets' proposal for a linkage called Christian Bridge.

As "guests of the president," our group received VIP treatment: a televised airport reception by government officials, private tours of the Kremlin museums (they literally shut the doors and locked other tourists out), accommodations in one of Moscow's most luxurious hotels, daily feature coverage in the national media, and an itinerary that included meetings with Gorbachev, the Supreme Soviet, *Pravda*, the KGB, Raisa Gorbachev's Culture Fund, the Academy of Social Sciences, and the Journalists' Club. One television producer told us, "Only Armand Hammer has received such treatment here, with access to so many places."

Some members of our delegation came with specific agendas: to obtain official sanction for their religious broadcasts, to speed the process of publishing Christian literature, to establish Christian study programs. We all hoped our meetings would help promote Christian work in general. Gradually, however, it became clear that we were not "using" the Soviet officials nearly so much as they were using us. Five years earlier, most of the activities of evangelical Christian organizations would have been illegal; now the government was reaching out to those same organizations in a desperate attempt to stave off anarchy and societal collapse. The revolution had come that far.

In this communal room, no one is ever bored,
For in the most visible place hangs the portrait of Lenin.
To you, happy children, he opens the whole world,
He looks at us with a big smile, as if about to speak.
Be happy, little ones,
Grandchildren of the October Revolution.

—SOVIET NURSERY SCHOOL SONG

CHAPTER 3

Rumblings from a Volcano

I EXPERIENCED A RUDE awakening in the Soviet Union, an empire I had always viewed as a threat to take over the world. Granted, its huge stockpile of nuclear weapons posed a unique threat, but who spread the alarming reports that the Soviet economy would soon catch up to the West? Certainly no one who has ever visited there.

My process of disabusal began on the trip over with stories about Aeroflot, the national airline. One veteran of thirty-two Aeroflot flights told me of her surprise on looking down and seeing the runway beneath her feet. Someone had neglected to patch a hole in the fuselage. When she alerted the flight crew, they seemed unconcerned about the outside air rushing in. "See, the windows leak too," they pointed out as if to reassure her. "We won't fly high enough for cabin pressurization to be a problem."

When the plane climbed, ice formed in the overhead baggage rack; when it descended, the ice melted, dousing her. She also had no seat belt.

As our plane dipped below the cloud cover on its initial approach into Moscow, I saw black highways threading a design in the late-October snowscape, but where were the vehicles? Comparable highways in Ohio or Pennsylvania would have been clogged with traffic. Eventually I found the vehicles: they formed a line eight blocks long, motors idling, waiting for gasoline.

Once inside Moscow's international airport I asked a question that would often occur to me, "When will they turn on the lights?" Can an entire airport be lit with a single forty-watt bulb? A local explained that Russia was running short of light bulbs.

On the drive into town, two things stood out: shabby construction and long lines of people at every storefront. What kind of society requires all its citizens, plumbers and nuclear physicists alike, to spend two hours a day standing in line? They are herded from place to place like farm animals and made to stand in orderly rows, waiting, waiting, always waiting, for goods no one would buy if they had any other choice.

A weirdly insulated Third World-level economy rests on the backs of an educated, cultured citizenry, all of whom seem clinically depressed. First under serfdom, then under communism, the Russian people have been beaten down. Samuel Johnson once remarked to Boswell, on passing a beggar, "I suppose it's better to have a society in which some are unhappy than one in which none are happy—which would be the case if perfect equality existed." Soviet communism never achieved its goal of perfect equality, but it did achieve the side effect Johnson predicted. An entire nation has lost its smile.

"Adam and Eve were Russian, you know," begins one joke Russians used to tell on themselves. "It's a logical deduction. They were improperly clothed, possessed only one apple between them, and someone was always telling them they lived in paradise!" Today, the joke needs revising—no one is telling the Russians they live in paradise. No one would dare. A cloud of impending doom hangs in the air.

A visitor gets the feeling of touring an active volcano. Smoke plumes curl from the top, red lava jets out a few places on the sides, but from down deep comes an ominous warning that the entire mountain may soon blow.

The danger is easily sensed beneath the crust of daily life. One day I went shopping. In the Melodia record store in downtown Moscow I chose ten classical albums: a fine selection of piano music, Russian liturgies, and chamber orchestra works, all featuring world-class performers. I waited in three lines, as always: one to place my order, one to pick it up, and one to pay. The bill for the ten albums came to forty rubles—about eighty-five cents at the official exchange rate. ("Did you check to see if they have grooves?" asked another member of our group when I returned to the hotel and announced my prize.)

I invited a friend out to lunch. We chose one of the new free-enterprise grills to ensure better quality and service, knowing the prices would be triple those of a state-run restaurant. After a twenty-minute wait in line, we ordered two of everything on the menu: steak, green beans, cranberries, bread and butter, caviar, dessert, beverage. The total came to forty-three cents—for both of us.

Such an economy cannot last. No one can even print a record jacket for eight-and-a-half cents, much less press a record. No one can grow a twenty-cent steak. A twilight zone economy based on the ruble is now colliding with the economic realities of the rest of the world. Within the insulated Soviet system, the prices make sense. For a middle-class Russian earning 300–400 rubles per month, my ten albums would represent a few days' salary. But because of government subsidies, prices bear no relation to the actual cost of the products. Soviets pay three rubles for a gallon of gasoline. Meanwhile, an imported pair of Nike running shoes goes for 2,500 rubles, more than six months' salary.

Every month the ruble continues its free fall in the world exchange. At the time of our visit the Union was disintegrating, and various republics outside Russia were printing money around the clock as fast as the presses could run. They cared not whether the ruble collapsed, since most republics planned to have their own currencies in place before long. Alongside the volcano, the ground trembled.

And yet despite all these problems it would be a gross distortion to depict only fear and gloom, for a visitor to the Soviet Union senses far more. Freedom has exploded like a shell burst.

"Throw open the heavy curtains which are so dear to you—you who do not suspect that the day has already dawned outside!" said Solzhenitsyn in 1969. Nowadays, everyone with eyes can see the bright light of dawn. Solzhenitsyn, once proclaimed a traitor and exiled, is now an honored citizen. Cite him in any gathering of intellectuals or even government bureaucrats and heads will nod affirmatively. Sometimes, spontaneous applause breaks out.

"I never thought this could happen, this revolution," said one former dissident. "We are like children waking from a nightmare in the middle of the night. All we want is reassurance that the nightmare won't happen again." No one can give that reassurance for the future, but in 1991, at least, the atmosphere was exhilarating. Everywhere—the newspapers, Radio Moscow, vendor stalls, restored churches, street preachers—signs of the new freedom abounded. Our very presence in Moscow, as North American Christians invited to advise the government on spiritual issues, was a token of the new dawn.

It's God that's worrying me. That's the only thing that's worrying me. What if He doesn't exist? What if Rakitin's right—that it's an idea made up by men? Then, if He doesn't exist, man is the chief of the earth, of the universe. Magnificent! Only how is he going to be good without God? That's the question.

—Fyodor Dostoevsky
The Brothers Karamazov

CHAPTER 4

Church Bells in the Kremlin

It would be hard to overstate the chaos we found in the Soviet Union, a nation that was about to shed its identity as well as its name. One day the central bank ran out of money. A few days later Ukraine, the second largest Soviet republic, seceded. A sense of crisis pervaded everything. Doctors announced the finest hospital in Moscow might close its doors in a month—no more cash. Crime was increasing almost 50 percent a year. No one knew what the nation would look like in a year or even six months. Who would control the nuclear weapons? Who would print the currency?

Perhaps because of this chaos, the Supreme Soviet seemed delighted to meet with our delegation. After a full day of listening to rancorous complaints from breakaway republics, an evening with nineteen foreign Christians probably seemed like a recess period.

When the letter proposing Project Christian Bridge went out in September 1991, the Supreme Soviet was the highest governing body in the nation, comparable to the US Congress. By the time we arrived in Moscow, though, barely a month later, no one seemed sure what the Supreme Soviet was supposed to be doing. Five of the twelve republics had not bothered to send delegates. Most major decisions were being handed down as presidential decrees from Mikhail Gorbachev or, more significantly, from Boris Yeltsin of the Russian republic.

We met with twenty committee chairmen and deputies in the Grand Kremlin Palace, a huge building constructed in the first half of the nineteenth century as a residence for the tsars. The palace, with its chandeliers, frescoed hallways, parquet floors, and decorative plaster moldings, still conveys a fine sense of grandeur. (On the way to the meeting we passed a park where stooped-over Russian women swept snow from the sidewalks with crude brooms of hand-tied straw. The contrast, in an egalitarian state, was stunning.)

The two groups, Supreme Soviet deputies and North American Christians, faced each other across long wooden tables. One end of the meeting room was dominated by a massive painting, in socialist realist style, of Lenin addressing a group of workers in Red Square. His face wore a severe, clench-jawed "we will right the world" expression.

Some of us could hardly believe the deputies' warm welcome. From these very offices in the Grand Kremlin Palace, over the past seventy years, other Soviet leaders had directed a campaign against God and religion unprecedented in human history. They stripped churches, mosques, and synagogues of religious ornaments, banned religious instruction to children, and imprisoned and killed priests. The government opened forty-four anti-religious museums, and published a national newspaper called *The Godless*.

Using government funds, first the League of Militant Atheists and then The Knowledge Society organized "unevangelism" campaigns of lectures and personal witnessing, with the specific aim of stamping out all religious belief. Vigilantes known as the "Godless shock brigades" went after the most stubborn believers. Until the fall of 1990, rigorous atheism had been the official doctrine of the Soviet government.[1] Now, exactly a year later, nineteen evangelical Christians were sitting across the table from the present leaders.

---

1. The USSR Freedom of Conscience Law, adopted in October 1990, formally abolished restrictions on religious faith. Article 5 represents the most dramatic change in policy: "The state does not fund religious organizations or activity associated with the propaganda of atheism." Government sponsorship of atheism campaigns were now illegal.

Konstantin Lubenchenko, chairman of the Supreme Soviet, introduced his side of the table, joking amiably as he came to his vice-chairman, a Muslim from the republic of Azerbaijan: "He follows Muhammad, not Jesus. Who knows, someday we may find out we all serve the same God." The vice-chairman, who looked like a Turkish bodybuilder squeezed into a suit two sizes too small, did not smile.

Lubenchenko is a handsome man with an expressive, strong-boned face. He wore his hair swept back from his forehead as if he had run a brush through it once, taking no time for a part. He was gregarious and witty, often interrupting his fellow deputies with jokes and repartee.

Nine months before, as a newly elected deputy Lubenchenko had visited the United States to observe democracy in action. He booked a room at the Washington Sheraton the week of the National Religious Broadcasters' Convention, one of the largest gatherings of evangelical Christians. As he stood in the lobby, adrift in a foreign land whose language and customs he did not know, the wife of Alex Leonovich, an NRB delegate, overhead him speaking Russian. The Leonoviches introduced themselves to Lubenchenko. They and Mikhail Morgulis, a Russian émigré, escorted the Soviet visitor around the capital, and invited him to the next day's Presidential Prayer Breakfast, where an awed Lubenchenko met President George H. W. Bush and other government leaders.

A friendship developed between Lubenchenko and some American Christians, and it was mainly through these contacts that Christian Bridge had come about. Just one week before our visit, the Supreme Soviet elected Lubenchenko as its chairman, which guaranteed us a cordial reception.

Our meeting with the deputies opened with brief statements from both sides. Our group, well aware of the ardent anti-religious policies pursued by this state government for many years, began rather tentatively. We spoke up for freedom of religion, and asked for the right to distribute Bibles and broadcast religious programs without restrictions.

Lubenchenko waved these opening remarks aside, as if to say, You're preaching to the converted here. "We need the Bibles very much," he said. "Is there a way to distribute them free instead of charging, so more people can get them?" I stole a glance at the mural of Lenin, wondering what he would have thought of these developments in his motherland.

After a few more comments John Aker, a pastor from Rockford, Illinois, spoke up. In preparation for this visit, our delegation members had urged each other to avoid any tone of triumphalism. We should approach the Soviets with respect, not offending them with direct references to the failures of their country. We should be honest about the weaknesses of the United States in general and the American church in particular. In that spirit John Aker remarked on the resurgence of the Soviet church.

"Returning home from my last visit to your country, I flew over the city of Pittsburgh just as the sun was setting to the west," he said. "It was a beautiful sunset, and I photographed it from the window of the plane. As I did so, I realized that the sun was just then rising in the Soviet Union. Going down in America, but coming up on the Soviet Union.

"Please don't be fooled by us tonight. I believe in many ways the sun seems to be going down on the church in America. We have taken too much for granted in our country and we have grown complacent. But I believe the sun is rising on the church here. Re-examine your history. Examine your spiritual legacy. And I pray you will lead your people in that light."

The deputies would have none of it. One commented wryly, "Perhaps the setting sun does not symbolize the decline of the Western church, but rather the sinking of communism in Russia!" Other deputies laughed loudly. Lubenchenko identified the speaker as a major-general in charge of the Ministry of State Security.

The general continued, "In the past weeks I have been negotiating reductions in strategic nuclear weapons. I have attended many meetings with my American counterparts. The cuts we have made will make our world more secure, I believe. And yet I must say that this meeting with you Christians tonight is more important for the long-term security of our nation than the meeting between our nation's presidents on eliminating nuclear weapons. Christianity can contribute much to our security as a people."

I checked the translation with the delegate beside me, who spoke Russian. Yes, I had heard right. The general really had said our meeting was more important than the START talks. A deputy from Belarus jumped in with warm praise for Christians who had responded so quickly with help for the victims of the Chernobyl disaster. Other deputies nodded assent. Another Soviet asked about the possibility of opening Christian colleges in the USSR.

Our group began to detect a pattern that would become increasingly evident throughout our trip. Whenever we tried to inject a note of realism, our Soviet hosts would cut us off. They looked at the United States, with all its problems, as a shining light of democracy; they saw the Christian church as the only hope for their demoralized citizens.

The Soviet leaders voiced a fear of total collapse and anarchy unless their society could find a way to change at the core, and for this reason they had turned to us for help. Somewhere in government files there must exist a profile of American evangelicals: good citizens, by and large; don't meddle too much in politics; support their leaders; strong work ethic. That citizen profile is sorely lacking in the USSR. And if God must come as part of the package, well, all the better.

One deputy quizzed us on the relationship between democracy and religion. "There is a direct tie," we responded. "Democracy is based on a belief in the inherent dignity of men and women that comes from their being created in the image of God. Furthermore, we also believe that governments are given divine authority to administer justice. In that respect, you leaders are agents of God." The deputies seemed to like that thought.

In general the Soviet deputies seemed bright, earnest, and deeply concerned about the problems outside the Grand Kremlin Palace. Most were young and energetic—a good thing, since they had been meeting thirteen hours straight that day—and I thought it a shame that these deputies would likely find themselves shut out of politics as the Soviet Union continued to unravel.

As the evening grew late, Lubenchenko asked one of the youngest deputies, an attractive woman in charge of cultural affairs, to sum up the new attitude toward religion. "I am impressed with how freely you can talk about your faith," she said, softly but with deep emotion. "I envy you! We have all been raised on one religion: atheism. We were trained to believe in the material world and not God. In fact, those who believed in God were frightened. A stone wall separated these people from the rest.

"Suddenly we have realized that something was missing. Now religion is open to us, and we see the great eagerness of young people. I envy those young people growing up today who can study religion. This is a hard time for us, when our ideals have been destroyed. We must explore religion, which can give us a new life, and a new understanding about life."

When she finished, Mikhail Morgulis, the organizer of our trip, asked if we could stand and pray. Television cameramen switched on banks of lights and roamed the room, poking their camera lenses into the faces of praying Soviet deputies, drinking in this strange sight for the benefit, and probable bewilderment, of Soviet television viewers.

On our way out we posed with our hosts for photos in the great hall, and I could not help noticing a bookstand display featuring the *Jesus* film and copies of the Bible in Russian. What had happened to the atheistic state? The change in attitude was unfathomable. I doubted whether the US Congress would have invited these same evangelical leaders to consult with them on spiritual and moral values, and I certainly couldn't remember seeing Bibles for sale in the US Capitol building.

We exited the Grand Kremlin Palace, and a chorus of bells rang out in the clear October air. The Revolution had silenced all church bells until a decree from Gorbachev made it legal for them to sound again. I saw an old woman wearing a *babushka* kneeling before a cathedral in prayer, an act that would have required immense courage a few months before. The irony struck me: within the walls of the Kremlin—officially atheistic until 1990—stand five separate gold-domed cathedrals. Is there another seat of government in all the world so crowded with churches?

A guide had pointed out a brick gate in the Kremlin wall still referred to as the "Savior Gate." It got its name from a large gilded frame mounted above the opening in the wall. Before the Revolution the frame held a painting of Jesus; since then, it has hung empty.

I looked at my watch, still set on Chicago time. It was October 31, Reformation Day. The Reformation had not penetrated the borders of Russia, in the sixteenth century or any other century. Now, in the least likely of all places, at the least likely of all times, there were unmistakable signs of spiritual awakening. "It's enough to make you a post-millennialist," muttered one member of our group.

Those men, so powerful,
always shown somewhat from below by crouching cameramen,
who lift a heavy foot to crush me,
no, to climb the steps of the plane,
who raise a hand to strike me,
no, to greet the crowds obediently waving little flags,
those men who sign my death warrant,
no, just a trade agreement
which is promptly dried by a servile blotter . . .

—STANISLAW BARANCZAK
"THOSE MEN SO POWERFUL"

CHAPTER 5

Praying with the KGB

SEVERAL TIMES IN MOSCOW we passed the sturdy pedestal that, until the failure of the August coup, had supported a statue of the founder of the secret police. Toppling the statue required the use of a huge crane, and for several days the workmen let the statue of Feliks Dzerzhinsky dangle from a steel-cable noose high above the street, a shocking symbol of the triumph of freedom over fear.

"The suspended statue reminded me of an oversized crucifix, like you see in South American cities," recalled one observer. "Only this martyr was the destroyer, not the Savior, of our people." By the time we arrived Dzerzhinsky had been dumped unceremoniously in a park by the Moscow

River, but Muscovites were still filing solemnly past the bare pedestal, staring at the vacant space, shaking their heads in disbelief.

We too shook our heads in disbelief when we got a friendly invitation to stop by the squat, hulking KGB building behind the pedestal and sip tea with the organization's leaders. Most of us had read dissidents' memoirs that describe in hideous detail what went on inside Lubyanka, the most famed and feared of Moscow's many prisons. From offices above that basement prison the KGB had overseen a vast network of prisons—several of which accommodated over one million inmates—exposed by Solzhenitsyn as "the gulag archipelago."

I felt long-buried rancor rush to the surface as we discussed our visit to the KGB. Cautious historians put the death toll from the camps and purges at ten to twenty million; Solzhenitsyn reckons the figure at sixty to seventy million. I can hardly comprehend these numbers, but I recoil in disgust against accounts of simple human cruelty inflicted by the KGB.

Andrei Sakharov, a dissident physicist, records that agents put cockroaches in his mail envelopes, punctured tires, smeared windows with glue, stole his dental bridges, glasses, and toothbrush. Solzhenitsyn writes of a friend who got a twenty-five-year prison sentence for attending the secret reading of a novel. It is rare to meet a Russian whose family has not been directly affected by KGB cruelty. Now we were to sip tea with the authors of such brutishness?

Some in our group, veterans of Iron Curtain days, had told us stories of harassment by KGB informers, and we had joked about wiretaps in our hotel, formerly the nest of the Central Committee of the Communist Party. That very day a man had approached two of us on Red Square and asked a few harmless questions, feigning drunkenness. We met him again in the lobby of the KGB building; recognizing us, he turned and ducked into a hallway. Unlike the statue of its founder, the KGB had not simply disappeared.

And, though toppled from his pedestal outside, even Feliks Dzerzhinsky lived on inside the KGB headquarters. The room we met in had a large photo of him still hanging on one wall, along with the obligatory photo of Lenin. The wood-paneled room was arranged like a small auditorium, with long tables oriented toward a speaker's table at the end. A handful of KGB agents, their faces as blank and impassive as their movie stereotypes, stood at attention by the doorway.

An aide to Gorbachev made a few opening remarks. "This is an amazing scene," he said to us. "You are helping to start a Christian revolution in this country, turning the thoughts of our government toward God. You are like a stone on the waters, and the ripples you stir up here will make it easier for others to follow." He then introduced General Nikolai Stolyarov, a KGB vice chairman in charge of all personnel.

We nodded in gratitude, but not without doubts in that setting. What impact can a stone have on a frozen lake? In his introductory statement, General Stolyarov did his best to dispel our doubts. A young, handsome man with a strong-boned face, Stolyarov had emerged as a popular hero during the August 1991 coup. A career officer in the Air Force, he had, at the height of the tension, flown to Gorbachev's *dacha* (summer house) to help rescue him. The KGB job was his reward.

Stolyarov began with an image obviously chosen for his religious audience, one that jarred us coming from a senior KGB official. "When the coup took place, it was as if the body of Christ had been taken, then resurrected. Our president was dead, and then alive again. I felt as if I had traveled all my life in the direction of that one moment. I was amazed at the peace I found at the moment of crisis, and amazed that I did not even have to use the gun at my side at such a time."

He went on for a few moments, detailing his actions against the coup. "Meeting with you here tonight," he concluded, "is a plot twist that could not have been conceived by the wildest fiction writer." Indeed. Stolyarov then opened the floor for questions.

What was his attitude toward Christians and Christian work? someone queried. "How to bring peace and quiet to the hearts of people is a great problem for us," the general replied. "We are united with you in working together against the powers of evil." A few looks were exchanged around the room, and eyebrows arched upward. I thought cynically of the cockroaches in Sakharov's envelopes and the humiliating strip search of Solzhenitsyn in the prison below.

Stolyarov continued, "We here in the USSR realize that too often we've been negligent in accepting those of the Christian faith. August 1991 shows what can happen. Seventy-four years ago we started with destruction, and now we are ending with destruction. Over the years we have destroyed many things of value. Now we have the problem: What to do next? The work of the KGB is familiar to you, of course, but now we have stopped our former existence. We are reorganizing. We have given some of our former authority to others."

He proceeded along this line, following a script that could have been written by Solzhenitsyn himself. "It is our capacity for *repentance*, not thinking, that differentiates us from the rest of animal creation," said Solzhenitsyn, and that is the improbable word Stolyarov turned to. "Political questions cannot be decided until there is sincere repentance, a return to faith by the people. That is the cross I must bear. I have been a member of the Party for twenty years. In our study of scientific atheism, we were taught that religion divides people. Now we see the opposite: love for God can only unite. Somehow we must learn to put together the missionary role—absolutely critical for us now—and also learn from Marx that man can't appreciate life if he is hungry."

Suddenly our heads were spinning. Was that "missionary role" he said? Where did he learn the phrase "bear a cross"? And the other word . . . *repentance*? Did the translator get that right? What to make of this never-never land in which the KGB leader now sounds like a seminarian? I glanced at Peter and Anita Deyneka, banned from the country for thirteen years, their visas always rejected because of their Christian activity, now munching cookies in the KGB headquarters. Hearing Stolyarov's words in the original Russian, and then in the English translation, they still could hardly believe them.

Stolyarov could not get off the hook so easily. Joel Nederhood, a refined, gentle man who makes radio and television broadcasts for the Christian Reformed Church, stood with a question. "General, many of us have read Solzhenitsyn's report of the gulag. A few of us have even lost family members there." His boldness caught some of his colleagues off guard, and the tension in the room noticeably thickened. "Your agency, of course, is responsible for overseeing the prisons. How do you respond to that past, and what changes have you put in place now?"

"I have spoken of repentance," Stolyarov replied in measured tones. "This is an essential step. You probably know of Abuladze's film by that title. There can be no *perestroika* apart from repentance. The time has come to repent of that past. We have broken the Ten Commandments, and for this we pay today."

I had seen *Repentance* by Tengiz Abuladze, and Stolyarov's allusion to it was no less startling than if he had cited Joseph McCarthy. The movie depicts false denunciations, forced imprisonment, the razing of churches—the very acts that had earned the KGB its reputation for cruelty in general and persecution of religion in particular. In Stalin's era an estimated 42,000 priests lost their lives. Ninety-eight of every one hundred Orthodox churches were shuttered. *Repentance* portrays these atrocities from the vantage point of one provincial town.

In the film's most tender scene, women of the village rummage through the mud of a lumberyard inspecting a shipment of logs that has just floated down the river. They are searching for messages from their imprisoned husbands who cut these logs in a labor camp. One woman finds initials carved into the log and, weeping, caresses it lovingly as a thread of connection to a husband she cannot caress. The movie ends with a peasant woman asking directions to a church. Told that she is on the wrong street (one named after a Stalinesque dictator), she replies, "Then what's the use of it? What good is a road that doesn't lead to a church?"

Now, sitting in the state headquarters of tyranny, in a room built just above the Lubyanka interrogation rooms, we were being told something very similar by the vice chairman of the KGB. What good is a path that doesn't lead to repentance, to the Ten Commandments, to a church?

Someone asked Stolyarov about the KGB's close relationship with the Orthodox Church. He acknowledged the problem immediately, admitting his organization had used priests as informers and had planted their own personnel in key positions. "Our government too often ended up abusing the constitution rather than protecting it," he said. "I am cutting out these activities right away."

Without warning, the meeting took a more personal turn. John Aker stood up. "General Stolyarov, I am a pastor from Rockford, Illinois. I began a career as an Army officer, and was trained as an Army Intelligence Agent. I taught courses in Soviet Bloc propaganda, and participated in two high-level counter-espionage activities that involved KGB officers.

"I grew up as a young boy in America very much afraid of the Soviet Union. That fear turned into distrust and finally, as an Army officer, it turned into hate.

"General, I feel very privileged to be here tonight. You said something that touched a chord deep within me. I have one thing to add, though. You used the phrase, 'That is the cross I must bear.' I went through a time when guilt over what I had done as an Army Intelligence Agent was destroying me. I couldn't bear that guilt, and I seriously considered ending my life.

That's when I realized I did not have to bear that cross forever. Jesus bore it for me.

"Jesus' love for me has in turn given me a love for the people of the Soviet Union. This is my fourth visit in six months, and I have found them to be loving, kind, and searching people. General, I mean it sincerely when I say that as I think of you, I will pray for you."

John Aker sat down, and General Stolyarov gave a brief response. "I am deeply touched by your words. They coincide with my own feelings, too. In coming to this position—even here right now with the KGB—I determined that I would never use force in dealing with people. With every power that is in me, I wish to turn the position into good."

Next, Alex Leonovich spoke. Alex had been sitting at the head table translating for Stolyarov. Of all the representatives selected for our delegation, Alex had the deepest personal investment in the outcome. A native of Belarus, he had escaped Stalin's reign of terror as a boy of seven, emigrating to the United States. After our week in Moscow he would remain behind, in hopes of returning to the town of his birth for the first time in sixty-two years.

For forty-six of those years Alex had been broadcasting Christian radio programs, often jammed, back to his homeland. He knew personally many Christians who had been tortured and persecuted for their faith. They wrote to him faithfully when his programs got through. For him, to be sitting next to a high official of the KGB translating such a message of reconciliation was both bewildering and nearly incomprehensible.

Alex is a stout, grandfatherly bear of a man with gray hair and a look of kindness imprinted in the wrinkles of his face. He epitomizes the old guard of warriors who have prayed, sometimes believing and sometimes not, for more than half a century that change might come to the Soviet Union—the very change we apparently now were witnessing. He spoke slowly and softly in Russian to General Stolyarov, and the Russian speakers scattered around the room translated quietly for the rest of us.

"General, many members of my family suffered because of this organization," Alex said. "I myself had to leave the land that I loved. My uncle, who was very dear to me, went to a labor camp in Siberia and never returned. I cannot possibly tell you what it means to me to hear these words tonight. My heart is full.

"General, you say that you repent. Christ taught us how to respond. On behalf of my family, on behalf of my uncle who died in the gulag, I want you to know that in the spirit of Christ I forgive you." And then Alex Leonovich, evangelist and president of Slavic Missionary Service, reached over to General Nikolai Stolyarov, vice chairman of the KGB, and the two embraced in a Russian bear hug.

Stolyarov whispered something to Alex, and not until later did we learn what he said. "Only two times in my life have I cried. Once was when I buried my mother. The other is tonight."

What was there left to do but pray? Our spokesman Mikhail Morgulis, a half-Jewish émigré whom Alex had befriended in New York and converted to Christ, rose to his feet and we all joined him. Mikhail prayed eloquently for "the thousands of our brothers and sisters who have perished," and for "the new leaders who would attempt to lead this nation down a new path." The television cameras clicked on, and cameramen vied for the best angle: American Christians praying underneath the photo of Dzerzhinsky, the KGB guards peeking nervously about the room, General Stolyarov wiping awkwardly at his face.

After the prayer, our delegation presented Stolyarov with a Bible, a children's Bible, and a translation of the works of C. S. Lewis. "I feel like Moses," Alex said on the bus home that evening. "I have seen the promised land. I am ready for glory." He chided himself for his lack of faith. To him, and to others, our visit with the KGB seemed a sacred moment distilled from the prayers of an entire generation and poured out of a crucible of suffering.

The local photographer accompanying us had a less sanguine view. "It was all an act," he said. "They were putting on a mask for you. I can't believe it." But he too wavered, apologizing a few minutes later: "Maybe I was wrong. Maybe they have changed. I don't know what to believe anymore."

The next day's *Izvestiya*, a newspaper with a circulation of eight million, featured a story with the headline "First prayer at Lubyanka." Our visit, the article said, coincided with the official day designated for the memory of those who died in the labor camps. We listened to a translation of the glowing report on our visit, and afterward one member of our group made a poignant correction. "They got all the facts right but one. There have been many prayers at Lubyanka—down in the basement. This was merely the first to make the official record."

There is nothing as bitter as this moment when you go out to the morning roll call—in the dark, in the cold, with a hungry belly, to face a whole day of work. You lose your tongue. You lose all desire to speak to anyone.

—ALEKSANDR SOLZHENITSYN,
ONE DAY IN THE LIFE OF IVAN DENISOVICH

CHAPTER 6

Basil and the Journalists

EACH DAY, AS MEMBERS of our delegation assembled for planning and prayer, we tried to assimilate the swirl of change we were witnessing. Can it happen? Can not just a person but an entire nation change? Can the KGB reform? Before long, skepticism melted away. What transpired at the KGB headquarters was but one dramatic episode in a week that convinced us attitudes toward religion have undergone a seismic change in the former Soviet empire.

Almost overnight the Soviet Union has moved away from an official position of atheism and hostility to become perhaps the most open mission field in the world. Wherever we went, officials invited us to set up relief work, exchange programs, study centers, religious publishing ventures. We heard reports that Young Life was inheriting camps from the Young Communists, and that the Gideons were frantically trying to resupply Bibles to hotel rooms (guests kept stealing them). Twenty-five hundred Soviet radio stations were carrying James Dobson's *Focus on the Family* program—more than in the United States, Canada, and the rest of the world combined. Campus Crusade staff members were preparing a curriculum on Christianity for the public schools.

After listening to a parade of politicians and government leaders express admiration and respect for Christianity, it was easy to lose sight of how radically the nation had changed. Soviet leaders seemed far more receptive to Christian influence than, say, their counterparts in the United States. Could their predecessors have been so devilish? An unexpected visit from Basil brought a jarring reminder of what life had been like for Christians under the communist regime.

For years Basil, who lived in Moldova, had clandestinely tuned in to short-wave programs by Alex Leonovich and Mikhail Morgulis. He had even heard Alex speak in person once, and ever since had harbored a desire to meet Alex again. Basil first heard a news item about Christian Bridge on "Voice of America." Then, incredulous, he listened as the official national radio network gave reports of our meetings with the Supreme Soviet and the KGB. The new openness toward religion seemed so inconceivable to Basil that he got on a night train and made the fourteen-hour journey from Moldova to Moscow in order to see us.

Somehow Basil found out what hotel we were staying in. "It's the Oktyabrskaya—the one that used to belong to the Central Committee," he was told, and again he could hardly believe it. He showed up in the lobby early one morning, just as we were gathering to pray and to review the day's schedule.

Ron Nikkel of Prison Fellowship later said he could tell Basil had been a prisoner as soon as he walked into the room, because he stared down at the floor and avoided direct eye contact. Basil had broad, hulking shoulders and the rugged, weather-beaten features of a farmer. He looked ill at ease in a suit and tie.

Basil had a most peculiar smile: two front teeth on the top row were missing, and when he smiled gold fillings in the back molars gleamed faintly through the gap. He presented us with sacks of gorgeous purple grapes and golden apples, which he had handpicked and carried on his lap from Moldova. He asked for five minutes to address us.

When Basil opened his mouth and the first sound came out, I jumped. We were meeting in a small room, and Basil spoke at the decibel level of a freight train. I have never heard a louder voice from any human being. We soon learned why.

In 1962 Basil founded a small publishing company with his own funds. He printed gospel tracts, distributing a total of 700,000 before the KGB paid him a visit. They demanded that he stop, and when he refused they arrested him and sent him to a labor camp. At first Basil was perplexed. Why should he be punished for serving God? What use could he be in a labor camp? But then one morning he saw in a flash that God had provided a new opportunity.

Every morning before sunup prisoners from the labor camp had to assemble in an open space for roll call. Camp commanders insisted on strict punctuality from prisoners, but not from guards, and so thousands of prisoners stood outdoors several minutes each morning with nothing to do. Basil, who loved to preach, decided to start a church.

As he was recounting this story in the hotel room, Basil spoke louder and faster, gesturing passionately with his arms like an opera singer. Every few sentences the translator, Alex, grabbed Basil's flailing arm and asked him to please slow down and lower his voice. Each time Basil apologized, looked down at the floor, and began again in a pianissimo that within three seconds crescendoed to a fortissimo. His voice had no volume control, and the reason traced back to that early morning scene in the labor camp.

Basil preached daily to a truly captive audience. Typically, he had about two minutes before the guards arrived, rarely as long as five minutes, and as a result it took up to two weeks to deliver a single sermon. He had to shout to be heard by several thousand prisoners, a strain that made him hoarse until his voice adapted. Over the years—ten years in all—of preaching outdoors to thousands, he developed the habit of speaking at top volume and breakneck speed, a habit he could never break.

Basil completed his sentence in 1972 and devoted his energies to building an unregistered church in his village. Sometimes he visited the church among the convicts and, he proudly reported, even today a community of one hundred believers still worships in that labor camp.

Basil's difficulties did not end with his release from prison, though. He told us of harassment by the authorities over his unregistered church, of the threats and public slanders and repeated vandalism of the church building. Finally, after nineteen years, opposition had faded away and he had just laid the last cement block and covered the church with a roof. He had come to Moscow, he said, to thank us for all we were doing, to bring us fresh fruit from Moldova, and to ask Alex Leonovich to speak at the dedication of his church.

"There were many years when I had no encouragement," Basil said. By now he was weeping openly and his voice cracked but did not drop one decibel. "The words of this man, Brother Leonovich, I carried in my heart. He was the one who encouraged me when my hands were tied behind my back." Basil then reached over, grabbed Alex by the shoulders, and kissed him in the Russian style once, twice, fifteen times—one for each year, he said, that he had waited for Alex to return.

"And now, such changes, I can hardly believe them," Basil said in closing. "We have been through the valley of tears. When Billy Graham came in 1959 they let him appear on a balcony but not speak. To think that you are here in Moscow, the center of unbelief, able to talk and drink tea with the leaders of our country. It is a miracle! Brothers and sisters, be bold! With your wings you are lifting up children of the Lord. Where I come from the believers are praying for you at this minute. We believe your visit will help reach our country for God. God bless you all."

Suddenly, I burned with shame. Here we were: nineteen evangelical professionals who made a comfortable living from our faith sitting in one of the most luxurious hotels in Moscow. What did we know about the kind of bedrock faith needed in this nation of people who had endured such suffering? What gave us the right to represent the Basils of the land before Mikhail Gorbachev and the Supreme Soviet, let alone the KGB?

We stood and prayed with Basil, and then he left. Later that day Alex Leonovich traded in his airplane ticket, incurring a huge penalty, in order to extend his stay. "How could I possibly turn down Basil's invitation?" he said. Our group went off to be feted in grand style with a banquet at the Ukrainian Embassy, and we did not see Basil again until later in the evening.

I looked forward to the event scheduled for that evening, a visit to the Journalists' Club. The inordinately polite reception we were receiving in Moscow was making me nervous. I knew that an entire atheistic state had not warmed to Christianity overnight, and I longed for a dialogue of true substance. I wanted us to be challenged with hard questions about what difference Christianity could make in a country coming apart at the seams. I thought I could count on cynical, hard-bitten journalists to render such a challenge.

I thought wrong. This is what happened at the Journalists' Club of Moscow. First, we North American Christians, seated on a spotlighted stage in a small theater, introduced ourselves. Ron Nikkel, normally taciturn, was feeling rather expansive. "Winston Churchill said you can judge a society by its prisons," he began. "By that standard, both the USSR and the United States are tragedies. Our prisons are awful.

"I have been in prisons all over the world, and have talked to sociologists, behaviorists, and criminal justice experts. None of them know how to get prisoners to change. But we believe—and I have seen abundant proof—that Christ can transform a person from the inside out. Jesus, himself a prisoner, was executed, but he rose again. Now many prisoners are rising again, thanks to him."

Ron then mentioned a prisoner in India who had returned to jail scores of times over a twenty-one-year span. The criminal simply could not break the cycle, until he found Christ. Puzzled by his absence in court, the local magistrate visited the man's home and asked what had happened. "For the first time in my life, someone forgave me," the ex-prisoner answered.

The room fell silent, and then these "cynical, hard-bitten journalists" did something I would not have predicted in a thousand years. They broke into loud, prolonged applause. These are the probing questions they tossed at Ron: "What is this forgiveness? How can we find it? How do you get to know God?" Later, one of the Soviet journalists told us that his profession had a special affinity for prisoners, since many had served time themselves.

When his turn came, Kent Hill introduced himself as the president of the Institute on Religion and Democracy. Several journalists leaned forward attentively. "It is no accident that democracy thrives alongside religion," Kent said. "Democracy is built on principles of individual human dignity. Our own Declaration of Independence acknowledges some rights as 'inalienable'—they are 'endowed by their Creator.' This fact puts limits on the power that any political leader can seize." Again the journalists applauded. Their follow-up comments showed that for them any connection between religion and democracy was an altogether novel idea.

Evidently, the journalistic elite of Moscow would not be the ones to question our basic Christian beliefs. They seemed far more intent on grasping after them, as if grasping for rare secrets of life that had been concealed for seventy years. After all of us seated onstage had introduced ourselves, the journalists responded.

A distinguished-looking, silver-haired gentleman stood first, identifying himself as an editor of the *Literary Gazette*, which we knew to be one of the most prestigious journals in the Soviet Union. "No doubt you know of the problems in our country," he said. "I tell you, however, that the greatest problem is not that we don't have enough sausages. Far worse, we don't have enough ideas. We don't know what to think. The ground has been pulled out from under us. We thank you deeply for coming to our country and holding before us morality, and hope, and faith. It is beautiful to see you in this place. You represent exactly what we need."

The next speaker was his polar opposite, a dissident who specialized in writing political satire. Slovenly dressed, ungroomed and passionate, with a bald head but spectacular eyebrows that protruded at least two inches, he looked as if he had stepped straight from a Dostoevsky novel. This character spoke in a voice almost as loud as Basil's. He had a bad stutter—odd to hear in a foreign language—and just as he reached a climactic point he would hang up on a word. "You are our salvation, our only hope!" he shouted. "We had a lawful country, a society with religious beliefs, but that was all destroyed in seventy years. Our souls were su-su-su-sucked out. Truth was de-de-destroyed. In the last stage, which we have just lived through, even the c-c-c-c-communist morale was destroyed."

When a young journalist stood and headed for the exit, this firebrand turned on him in a fury, calling him down publicly. Finally, the emcee had to intervene and silence the stormy dissident. "I think our friend just went out for a smoke," he said. "Does someone else have a comment?"

A beautiful blonde woman wearing a red silk blouse and a leather skirt and matching boots made her way to the aisle. She stood just before the stage, her hands clutching a designer purse. I had not seen such fine clothes in Moscow. Mikhail Morgulis whispered to me that she was a popular newscaster—something like the Connie Chung or Diane Sawyer of Russia. "I am so shaken to be here tonight," she said, and then paused a moment to control her voice.

"I am shaking! I feel so blessed to learn that American leaders are concerned with spiritual and moral problems. I am a person educated in religion and yet I am only on the first step in understanding what is God. So many visitors have come here to make a profit in our country, but I am so thankful that the American *intelligentsia* care enough to come and meet with people at such important levels over these issues."

She was followed by others who rose to give a similarly embarrassing overassessment of our importance as a delegation. As in previous meetings, we tried to mention flaws in American society and in the American church, but the journalists seemed altogether disinterested in apologies or critiques. They seemed, rather, starved—grievously starved for hope.

I thought of the reception our group might get at the Press Club in Washington, DC, the questions we might prompt from the editors of *The New Republic* or *Esquire*. I tried to imagine Connie Chung or Barbara Walters being vulnerable before her peers, as this woman journalist had been. As I was mulling over these thoughts, I noticed in the audience a familiar figure in a peculiar green suit.

The theater lights had been dimmed for our introductions, but now that the audience was responding other lights were switched on. Sitting in the back row was Basil, he of the foghorn voice and the two-minute church in the gulag. From then on I kept one eye on Basil, wondering how an ex-convict from Moldova felt in such an environment among the celebrities of Moscow.

Whenever someone mentioned the word "God" or "Jesus," Basil raised both fists over his head, and even from the stage I could almost see the gleam in the gap between his teeth. On the back row, out of view of the audience, Basil was acting as our one-person charismatic cheerleading crew.

For the first time that day I glimpsed our group as Basil saw us: his ambassadors, going where he would not be invited, speaking words he could not always follow, opening doors he had thought sealed shut forever. We, too, those of us who felt so unworthy in his presence that morning, had a role to play.

Basil stood for millions of Soviet Christians who had lived out their faith in fear and trembling. Incredibly, the tables had turned. Now the journalists of Moscow applauded when they heard stories of converted prisoners, and craved news about God as a dying patient craves a miracle cure. They hung on our words about Christianity as Russian economists hung on words about capitalism, as if we were smuggling in a secret formula from the West that might salvage their land.

We were not bringing imports from the West, however. The God we served had been in Russia all along, worshiped hungrily in the camps and in the unregistered house churches and in the cathedrals the communists had not razed.

These journalists, all masters of Moscow's cocktail party circuit, had never met a simple saint like Basil. It was our job to introduce them.

All that the downtrodden can do is go on hoping. After every disappointment they must find fresh reason for hope.

—ALEKSANDR SOLZHENITSYN,
THE GULAG ARCHIPELAGO

CHAPTER 7

Interlude in Zagorsk

WE HAD ONE SUNDAY on our own in Moscow, and our delegation scattered to different churches. Partly because of comments by the journalists, I wanted to attend a Russian Orthodox church service.

In almost every meeting with our Soviet hosts, questions about the church had surfaced. No one questioned the need for religion, but everyone asked what kind of religion was needed. What did we think of the Russian Orthodox? Did we intend to cooperate with them? Did we think the Russian Orthodox capable of leading a national moral reform?

The wording of some of these questions betrayed the askers' suspicions. Some thought a history of coziness with the Communist Party had fatally compromised the powerful Russian Orthodox Church. One government minister put it bluntly: "The Orthodox Church has taken over the very worst aspects of communism."

The persistent questions led to some heated discussion within the ranks of our delegation. Those who had many years of experience working in the USSR tended to disparage the Russian Orthodox Church. "No group is more *opposed* to what we hope to accomplish," said one veteran. He had seen the church comply with the persecution of unregistered believers, and had watched with dismay as church officials mouthed the Party line at world religious gatherings.

Furthermore, what made us think the Russian Orthodox would be open to cooperation with evangelical groups? During our week in Moscow, the Church Patriarch refused to grant an audience to Pope John Paul II, who wished to visit Moscow, on account of the Catholics' penchant for proselytism. What would he think of the evangelical missionary movement?

In the end, though, our group agreed to avoid all criticism of the Russian Orthodox Church. We would identify ourselves as Protestant evangelicals, and stress our emphasis on the Bible. If questioned further we would reply that it is essential for all Christians—Catholics, Protestants, and Orthodox—to work together in meeting the country's spiritual needs. This decision seemed vindicated when the Patriarch, in all his pomp and ceremony, paid an official visit to the Russian Bible Society to mark its reopening. As a sponsoring partner, the Orthodox denomination had thrown its full weight behind the Bible Society.

Within our group Ron Nikkel, president of Prison Fellowship International, spoke most emphatically for cooperation. "The priests already have the respect of the people," he insisted. (Polls show that Soviets are eight times more likely to trust a religious leader than a political leader.) "They have resources, the loyalty of fifty million members, and a long tradition of spiritual authority. We must not try to work against them."

Ron said he had met many priests who demonstrated a deep spirituality and a genuine compassion for the people. When I asked to see an example of this compassion at work, Ron arranged a trip fifty miles northeast from Moscow to visit two sites: the Zagorsk Monastery, richest jewel of the Russian Orthodox Church, and the Zagorsk Prison, possibly the worst prison in the Soviet Union.

Ron and I stepped out of the hotel on a cold Sunday morning to look for Sasha's aging, clattery sedan of Russian make. Sasha, an engineer with a social conscience, had begun visiting the Zagorsk Prison two years before, making the long drive once a week. Initially he had only disdain for the Russian Orthodox Church, but encounters with the monks at Zagorsk changed his outlook, and recently Sasha had begun attending an Orthodox church in downtown Moscow.

Sasha was a thin, small man, with a long, pointed beard that any Russian priest might envy. A fitness buff, he went for a five-mile run every morning, followed by an invigorating swim in the Moscow River (except in deepest winter, when the ice grew too thick to chop through by hand). He had arisen at five that morning in order to complete his regimen.

Sasha understood English, but spoke little. For help with translation he had brought along his sixteen-year-old daughter Julia, a pretty, dark-haired girl with an athlete's build. I learned she was the second-ranked girls' tennis player in Moscow, and was hoping to win a scholarship from a college in Alabama. "Well, you see, I don't have so many clever brains," Julia said, apologizing for her obsession with sports. Her brains proved sufficiently clever to get us through some difficult translation.

We drove through Moscow along the river boulevard that runs beside the Kremlin complex. It was a startlingly clear day, temperature well below freezing, and the gold onion domes of the Kremlin cathedrals, glittering with ice crystals, shone like miniature suns against a deep blue sky. The river was blackened silver. In Red Square, long lines were already forming by Lenin's tomb and the fairy-tale spires of St. Basil's Cathedral. Sasha pulled to the curb to allow us to take in the view, one of the most breathtaking man-made sights in the world.

Drab gray suburbs outside Moscow soon yielded to rolling hills and birch forests. A light dusting of snow from the previous night gave the scenery a postcard-like quality. Among the trees we saw a few farmhouses from tsarist times, their decorative woodwork restored and painted with bright colors. After an hour of driving we came over a rise and there, spread out before us, was the monastery of Zagorsk.

Zagorsk is a feast for the eyes, a veritable Disneyland of sacred architecture. A cluster of fifty magnificent buildings that includes two cathedrals, numerous chapels, a tsar's palace, and a wood-frame hospital, the monastery showcases the finest architectural styles from the fifteenth to the seventeenth century. The largest cathedral was built by an Italian in Renaissance style. The most enchanting, Moorish in appearance, has four symmetrical blue domes that shimmer with inlaid gold stars. Monks keep the monastery grounds in spotless condition, and tree-lined walks lead from one architectural treasure to another. Zagorsk sheltered the last enclave of Russian civilization in the days of the Tatar invaders, and had long served as seat of the Russian Patriarch, the Pope of the East.

Brother Bonifato, a red-bearded priest dressed in flowing black robes, met our car at the gate and ushered us into the rococo Cathedral of the Assumption, where a service was underway. Ducking through a private side entrance, we immediately found ourselves in the front row of a small, vaulted chapel attached to the main cathedral. Before us loomed a wall that appeared covered with solid gold, inset with the five-tiered iconostasis. Ensconced candles lent a soft, eerie glow to the room, as if the walls were the source, rather than reflection, of light.

We stood beside a 150-voice choir composed entirely of young monks in training. (Zagorsk turns away three to four applicants for every candidate it admits.) The air hummed with the throaty, bass-clef harmony of the Russian liturgy, a sound that seemed to come from under the floor. After the choir had sung a few bars, they were answered antiphonally by a choir of equal size, hidden from view in another chapel.

The vaulting caused sound waves to bounce down on us again and again in harmonic overtones, creating an intense aural effect. That, combined with the scent of melting candle wax and burning incense, made for a very sensory service. I could easily understand the sentiments of Prince Vladimir's emissaries who in AD 988 had first recommended converting Russia's tribes to Christianity. Hearing this same liturgy on a visit to Constantinople, they reported back, "We knew not whether we were in heaven or on earth, for on earth there is no such splendor or such beauty."

The service seemed very Old Testament in style. Ancient Hebrews had no icons, of course, but Russian believers treated the iconostasis almost like an altar, lighting candles before it and using the icons as a focal point for meditation and supplication. As in the Old Testament, only priests were allowed behind the high altar where the elements were prepared. Periodically, priests wearing bejeweled robes and elaborate headdresses swept up and down the aisle in a glittering procession, swinging incense containers or holding up a Bible encased within a gold cover studded with precious stones.

An Orthodox service lasts three to four hours, with worshipers entering and leaving at will. The laity have little participation; a concept like "the priesthood of all believers" is utterly foreign. No one invites congregants to "pass the peace" or "greet the folks around you with a smile." They stand—there are no chairs or pews—and watch the professionals, who are very professional indeed. I caught a glimpse of the main cathedral area, packed with over two thousand worshipers, many of them younger than thirty.

The service had undeniable power, and it gave me an understanding of both the praise and criticism I had heard regarding the Orthodox Church. Admirers commended its spirit of reverence and worship. By carrying on a ritual virtually unchanged in a millennium, the church had given the Russian people a sense of stability and permanence unavailable elsewhere in their turbulent society. It had preserved the message of the gospel by enfolding it in pictures, songs, and imagery that any illiterate peasant could comprehend.

Critics, on the other hand, pointed out the irrelevance of the church. By adhering to a form based on liturgy dispensed by distant professionals, the church was perpetuating the vast societal gulf that had always divided Russia. People had no model of how to apply Christianity to daily life. Dostoevsky made this complaint forcefully in *The Brothers Karamazov*. The church relies on "miracle, mystery, and authority," said the Grand Inquisitor: the three temptations rejected by Christ in the wilderness, but adopted by the church ever since.

Bonifato, however, as well as Nikodim and several other brothers from the Zagorsk Monastery, were breaking the stereotypes of the Church of Irrelevance. From that sublime service Brother Bonifato led us straight to one of bleakest settings imaginable. "Really, it's a dungeon," Ron Nikkel warned as we traveled a mile to the Zagorsk prison. "Like you'd expect to find in Dickens's day. I haven't seen such conditions outside of Africa." Aware that Ron has toured prisons in scores of different countries, I braced myself for the worst.

I found the worst. Zagorsk prison, the oldest in Russia, was constructed in 1832, and the builders set its stone walls below ground to minimize the need for heating. To reach the prisoners' quarters, we went through four steel gates, down, down, down worn stone steps that led progressively toward the source of an acrid stench, the prisoners' cells on the bottom level.

The first cell we entered was ten feet by twelve feet, about the size of my bedroom in Chicago. Eight teenage boys—the youngest was actually twelve—jumped to attention when the door opened. The room held only four beds, so two boys slept on each bed. There was a rickety table, but no other furniture. Each boy had a plastic bag hanging from the end of his bed that contained one change of clothing, the only belongings permitted. A thin, soiled blanket covered each bed, but I saw no sheets or pillowcases.

In one corner of the room was a ceramic-lined hole in the ground with two footpads marked out for squatting. This hole, open to view on all sides, functioned as both toilet and "shower," although the only water came from a cold-water spigot an arm's length away. The basement cell had a single six-inch window, frosted over and welded shut, at the very top of one wall. A bare bulb dangled at the end of a wire descending from the ceiling.

There were no board games, no television or radio sets, no diversions of any kind. All day every day for a year, two years, maybe five, these boys had nothing to do but lie on their beds or pace around the room, waiting for freedom. Most of them, I learned, were serving time for petty theft.

The room had one bright spot of color: a crude, arched altar fashioned out of tinfoil adorned one wall, home for some tiny painted icons that Brother Nikodim had donated. He had also given the boys a supply of Christian books. Brother Bonifato introduced us to each youngster, moving easily among them, resting his hand on their shoulders as he talked.

The women's quarters were even worse. Bunks sticking out from the wall left an aisle barely wide enough to stand in. The women had no special amenities; their toilet and shower arrangements were exactly the same as the boys'.

When the steel door to one women's cell opened I could hardly see inside, the room was so thick with what looked like fog. We soon saw why. One of the women had rigged up a crude electrical contraption: by twisting a lamp cord wire around a live wire near the ceiling, she had managed to divert an electrical current. The lamp cord, crudely spliced in three places, fed current to a rusty electrical coil, which was heating water in a small tin basin. From the looks of the fog, the women kept the water boiling all day: it provided some heat for their stone-walled cell, and gave a source of hot water for bathing as well. Did they also make coffee out of that rusty brown water? I flinched at the thought.

For security purposes, Zagorsk observes a permanent twenty-four-hour lockdown. Prisoners don't take walks in the hallway, visit a cafeteria, or go outdoors to an exercise yard. Male and female, young and old, they sit in their tiny dungeon cells like animals, interrupted only by the food that comes once a day. They cannot even see into the hallway. A solid steel door seals off every cell, except for a tiny hinged grate that a guard can pull back to peer inside.

Yet when the prisoners spoke of their main worry, it concerned life outside the prison, not inside. Russia has always maintained a strict policy against hiring ex-convicts. As the law now stands, upon release, these prisoners will get a "convicted" stamp on their identity cards, which will make them ineligible for employment. Few have families to support them;

without income, what alternative do they have to stealing food or supplies and landing back in prison again?

The warden of this grim prison turned out to be a dedicated, even courageous man. In a country fast disintegrating, prison budgets get cut first. Two years before, when the government shut off his supplies of food, this warden approached the monks at the monastery for help. Out of their own storehouses, the monks donated enough bread and vegetables to feed the prisoners throughout the winter.

The monks' selfless response impressed the warden, a communist at the time. "I don't know where the country will go in the future," he told us. "Right now with all the changes in the KGB I don't even know who my boss is. Who can I write with my requests for aid? As for this place, we are turning back to our ancient roots in the church. Where else can we turn?"

The warden spoke candidly as we met in his office after our tour. He was responsible for six hundred prisoners and his dispensary contained not a single aspirin. He asked Ron for help in procuring antibiotics, bandages, and basic medical supplies.

Ron described a prison in Brazil run by Christians associated with Prison Fellowship, and the warden listened intently. He volunteered to go to Brazil and look it over, then report back to his superiors—after he found out who they were. The two discussed the possibility of Prison Fellowship assuming management of the worst prison in Russia to use it as a model of reform.

On his own, the warden had already asked the monks about moving some of the prisoners to one of the properties the government had recently returned to the church. Trusted prisoners could live there, do the work of restoration free of charge, and raise crops to feed their fellow prisoners back in Zagorsk.

In 1989 the warden had authorized the monks to rebuild a chapel in the prison basement—an act of remarkable boldness for a communist functionary in the atheistic state prevailing then. Just before leaving Zagorsk prison, Ron and I asked if we could see the result of their work.

Located on the lowest subterranean level, the chapel was an oasis of beauty in an otherwise grim dungeon. The priests had installed a marble floor, and mounted finely wrought candle sconces on the walls. Prisoners spent many hours cleaning out a seventy-year accumulation of filth from the room, which had been used as a storeroom. They took pride in their chapel, the only prison chapel, we were told, in all of Russia. Each week priests traveled from the monastery to conduct a service there, and for this occasion prisoners were allowed out of their cells, which naturally guaranteed excellent attendance.

We spent a few minutes admiring the handiwork that went into the room, and Brother Bonifato mentioned that the icon for the prison chapel was "Our Lady Who Takes Away Sadness." Ron commented that there must be much sadness within these walls, then turned to Brother Bonifato and asked if he would say a prayer for the prisoners. Brother Bonifato looked puzzled, and Ron repeated, "Could you say a prayer for the prisoners?"

"A prayer? You want a prayer?" Brother Bonifato asked, and we nodded. He looked thoughtful, then disappeared behind the altar at the end of the room. He brought out an icon of the Lady Who Take Away Sadness, which he propped up on a stand. Then he retrieved two candle holders and two incense bowls, which he laboriously hung in place and lit.

Ron and I looked at each other and rolled our eyes. We were already an hour late for a meeting back in Moscow. "Sorry," Ron whispered. "I guess extemporaneous prayer isn't in his repertoire."

Brother Bonifato was far from finished. He removed his headpiece and outer vestments. He meticulously laced gold cuffs over his black sleeves. He placed a droopy gold stole around his neck, and then a gold crucifix. He carefully fitted a different, more formal headpiece on his head. Before each action, he paused to kiss the cross or genuflect. Finally, he was ready to pray.

Prayer involved a new series of formalities. Brother Bonifato did not say prayers; he sang them, from a liturgy book propped on another stand. At one point he paused to teach us a few Russian sentences so we could join in. Finally, twenty minutes after Ron had requested a prayer for the prisoners, Brother Bonifato said "Amen," and we exited the prison into the wonderful fresh air outside.

The procedure in the prison chapel brought back for me the inner conflict I had felt while worshiping in the monastery cathedral that morning. Reverence, submission, awe, *mysterium tremendum*—the Russian Orthodox Church knew these qualities well, and conveyed them superbly in worship. But God remained faraway, approachable only after much preparation and only through intermediaries such as priests and icons.

I thought of the teenagers back in their basement cell. If one of them needed prayer, for the strength to endure or for a sick family member outside, would Brother Bonifato have followed the same ritual? Would the boys in the cell dare to think of approaching God themselves, praying in the casual and everyday language that Jesus used?

Yet there is no Prison Fellowship staff person to assign to Zagorsk—not yet anyway—no paid chaplains, Young Life, or Youth For Christ volunteers to send into the dungeon. There is only the monastery of the Russian Orthodox Church, which next to the government remains the most powerful institution in Russia. When the need arose, the monks had responded: with bread, with their incarnational presence, with the reinstitution of worship in the unlikeliest of places. I had seen the best and worst of Russia in one morning in Zagorsk, and for just a moment they had come together.

Do you know what astounds me most about the world? It is the
impotence of force to establish anything. . . .
In the end, the sword is always conquered by the mind.

—NAPOLEON

CHAPTER 8

Man of the Decade

DOSTOEVSKY WROTE, "A PERSON cannot live without worshiping something." On the drive back into Moscow, I noted a striking similarity between the religions of Russia's distant past and its recent past. An elaborate mausoleum at Zagorsk displayed the preserved body of Father Sergy, a great patriot and Russian saint, and pilgrims had come from miles around to touch or kiss the coffin. Those lines formed a mirror image of the lines we passed snaking out from Lenin's tomb in Red Square. The cathedral had rows of icons; the streets of Moscow had rows of statues. The Zagorsk Prison had Our Lady Who Takes Away Sadness; the KGB headquarters had (until recently) a monument to its founder, who had given the nation so much sadness. The communists had replaced a God-man with their own man-gods.

Those of us from a democratic tradition, accustomed to casual jokes about politicians, can hardly fathom the absolute power once wielded by Soviet leaders. Solzhenitsyn tells of a hapless workman who got ten years in prison for hanging his coat on a bust of Lenin, and of a woman who got ten years for carelessly scribbling a note on a newspaper over a picture of Stalin.

Another scene recorded in *The Gulag Archipelago* shows the outer limits of the cult of personality. The speaker at an obscure district Party meeting called for a tribute to Comrade Stalin (who was not even present). All rose for the obligatory applause, which rolled on and on until suddenly it dawned upon the assembled Party members that someone must be the first to stop clapping. No one dared. Applause went on for five minutes, nine, ten, eleven minutes. At last the manager of a local paper factory, tired and sore-palmed, quit slapping his hands together. He was promptly arrested and served ten years for showing disrespect to the Great Leader.

Against this background of despotism that had characterized all but a few years of the Soviet regime, Mikhail S. Gorbachev brought a wholly new style. It took years for the Soviet people to trust the new words, *glasnost* and *perestroika*, that suddenly dominated their vocabulary. It took the West even longer to trust the olive branches Gorbachev held out. Would he really allow the Berlin Wall to come down? Was he serious about nuclear disarmament? Ultimately, Gorbachev won over most skeptics. He was awarded a Nobel Peace Prize and designated *Time* magazine's "Man of the Decade."

At the time of our visit, Gorbachev still retained the title President of the Soviet Union, but no one knew what power that office held or indeed how much longer the term "Soviet Union" would have any meaning. (During our week in Moscow the red, white, and blue Russian flag conspicuously appeared over Kremlin buildings, replacing the red Soviet flag.) Throughout the trip, our promised meeting with Gorbachev hung in limbo, subject to such exigencies as the latest political crisis, his sudden trip to Madrid for the Middle-East Peace Conference, and the state of the economy. Our delegation hoped a meeting would take place, but we did not hear definite word until the Sunday night I returned from Zagorsk, a few days before our scheduled departure. By then we had received a good dose of Soviet cynicism about Gorbachev.

On Arbat Street the tourist trinket of choice was a "Gorby doll," a political takeoff on the Russian *Matryoshka* dolls. Traditional *Matryoshka* dolls, hand-painted on wood, portray a chubby-faced child in exquisite Russian costume. The doll breaks apart at the waist, and inside is an exact duplicate, only slightly smaller. That one also breaks apart, spilling out many identical dolls, each fitting snugly into the other, until at last the tiniest doll is uncovered. You see these dolls displayed everywhere in Moscow, their ten or eleven components lined up stair-step like a family of clones.

Gorby dolls vary the pattern. The smallest doll is a likeness of Marx, who is enclosed within Lenin, who is in turn swallowed up by Stalin, Khrushchev, and then Brezhnev. The largest doll will vary, depending on the artist's politics. Some feature Gorbachev on the outside, enclosing Yeltsin; some have Yeltsin enclosing Gorbachev. A few have Yeltsin's profile painted on the front of the largest doll, and Gorbachev's on the back—"twins, just alike," say the salesmen. The dolls communicate a less-than-subtle message: nothing much has changed. Faces may vary, but they're all communists of one form or another.

That simmering political cynicism may, ironically, be one of the surest signs that democracy is taking hold at the grassroots. At the least, it shows the decline of the absolute dictator.

It was with a high level of anticipation that we retraced our steps to the Kremlin to meet with Gorbachev. By then we had become well-acquainted with "the Russian style." We would gather in the hotel lobby at the appointed time, stand around for an hour or so, call the bus company about the no-show bus, wait for a replacement (typically, the driver of the original bus would not call in when his vehicle broke down), then wind our way through Moscow to the appointed place. Every meeting started well behind schedule, and involved long, flowery introductions. Only after much ceremonious talk did the discussion settle down to matters of substance.

Gorbachev was different. Our bus was late, as usual, and when we motored through the red brick Spassky Gate, presidential assistants met us on the run, gesturing wildly for us to hurry. A procession of evangelicals dressed in our best suits sprinted across cobblestone plazas and alleyways until we reached the presidential office complex, in an elegant hall built by the tsars. Security guards with two-way radios directed us to leave our overcoats—surprisingly, we went through no metal detectors or body frisks—and thirty seconds later we were escorted in, breathing heavily, to meet Gorbachev.

He shook hands with each member of the delegation, motioned us to our seats, and began precisely at eleven, as scheduled. A cortege of intense young men entered through a side door, bearing plates of biscuits and cups of tea served on state china. Clearly, Gorbachev had mastered the Western style of doing business. He gave an opening statement that showed he had been well briefed, and spoke right to the point, maintaining excellent eye contact the entire time.

"I have read your letter, and I thank you for it," he began.[1] "I found it very warm and moving. I do not get many such letters. Mostly I get letters from people who are worried. 'What is going to happen? Our country is in a difficult time,' they say. I share those worries. We are in a crisis, including a spiritual crisis, as the country undergoes so many changes so quickly.

"Civil strife and division are springing up everywhere. In the past change in my country has come with a circle of blood; now we are trying to bring about change democratically. If we succeed it will be good for all of us. But for the democratic process to work here, we will need a profound and systemic reform. Getting to that point is a very difficult challenge."

Gorbachev seemed vigorous and healthy. His skin looked tanned, thanks to the makeup he wore as a concession to the omnipresent cameras. He was fully in command.

"Let me be honest with you—I am an atheist," the president added, setting to rest all rumors about his being a closet believer. "I believe that man is at the center and must solve his own problems. That is my faith. Even so, I have profound respect for your beliefs. This time, more than ever before, we need support from our partners, and I value solidarity with religion. As you know, we have many important decisions to make, and this is a very busy day. The next hour, I am meeting with presidents of all the republics. But I felt it necessary to carve out this time with you. Raisa, my wife, assured me it was important!"

At this point Lubenchenko, chairman of the Supreme Soviet, broke in. "But," he said with a wink, "if the President finds betrayal repugnant, shows compassion for his fellow man, encourages freedom, respects the decency and rights of individuals, and has the goal of moving toward the good, then perhaps words don't matter so much. Perhaps by deeds he is a believer, if not by words."

Gorbachev laughed. "I do not object. I must say that for a long time I have drawn comfort from the Bible. Ignoring religious experience has meant great losses for society. And, I must acknowledge that Christians are doing much better than our political leaders on the important questions facing us. We welcome your help, especially when it is accompanied by deeds. My favorite line in your letter is, 'Faith without deeds is dead.'"

Joel Nederhood and Mikhail Morgulis responded on our behalf, in this fashion: "Mr. President, we support you. We honor you for taking the time to meet with us, and also for the many changes you have brought to

---

1. The letter stating the goals of Project Christian Bridge appears in the Appendix.

the world. You are in our prayers. We represent millions of Christians in North America who pray for you, and who have a long history of helping people in need. We will carry a message back to them, and do our best to direct aid to the Soviet Union—both spiritual and material aid. We believe the world is a safer and freer place because of you. We believe you have been chosen by God for your task."

At that last comment a Delphic smile crossed Gorbachev's face. "I am deeply moved," he said. "We are learning, though, that in a democratic country we need support not only from God but from the people!" He added a few comments about the August coup, and the need for his nation to punish the coup plotters while avoiding undue revenge.

As the meeting proceeded, Gorbachev grew more and more relaxed. He departed from his prepared notes, and seemed to welcome a more casual discussion. Mikhail Morgulis, taking note of this change, ventured, "Mr. President, perhaps this meeting itself is one of the best proofs of the existence of God. Christians have not always been so welcome in this room, and for more than a year I have been praying for this meeting to take place!" Gorbachev laughed and nodded approval. "Yes, yes, well, it has taken a long time, but it's important to have patience."

Gorbachev had promised us fifteen minutes and gave us almost forty. He stood respectfully as Morgulis led a brief prayer, posed for a few official photos, shook hands with us again, and hurried off to his luncheon with the presidents.

For some members of the group, the meeting with Gorbachev represented a high-water mark. More than any other event in the trip, it showed the profound change in the Soviet attitude toward Christians. A few days before, a government official had attended the reopening of the Russian Bible Society, an organization that had not been allowed to function for seventy years. "We have treated this book like a bomb," he said, holding up a Bible. "Like contraband material, we have not allowed Bibles into our country. Now we realize how wrong that was." Mikhail Gorbachev was in many ways personally responsible for the loosening the bonds that had restricted the practice of religion.

And yet other members of the group expressed disappointment after the meeting—not with Gorbachev, but with us. For nearly a week we had been praying that we not be dazzled by the trappings of power. "How would Jesus conduct himself in the halls of the Kremlin?" one member had challenged us. We agreed to leave all cameras behind, to observe the strictest protocol, to present Mr. Gorbachev with a Bible and downplay all other gifts. But when the meeting took place, the aura of fame proved overwhelming. For hours afterward, the group basked in the glow of having sat in the presence of one of the great men of the century.

Later that afternoon Gorbachev's office called to report that he had been most impressed with the goals of Christian Bridge. "My meeting with the presidents could have used some of that harmony and good spirit!" Gorbachev remarked. He asked permission to release the text of our mission statement to the Associated Press, along with photos of our meeting. In a lead article about our visit to Moscow, the Soviet newspaper *Izvestiya* made perhaps the best observation, "Truly the ways of the Lord are inscrutable."

The struggle against religion is not a campaign, not an isolated phenomenon, not a self-contained entity; it is an inseparable component . . . an essential link and necessary element in the complex of communist education.

—*Pravda*, January 12, 1967

If you meet with difficulties in your work, or suddenly doubt your abilities, think of him—of Stalin—and you will find the confidence you need. If you feel tired in an hour when you should not, think of him— of Stalin—and your work will go well. If you are seeking a correct decision, think of him—of Stalin—and you will find that decision.

—*Pravda*, February 17, 1950

CHAPTER 9

Fall from Grace

As a journalist, I eagerly anticipated a scheduled meeting with the staff of *Pravda*. The Soviet Union has little tradition of free speech or free press— until recently all photocopy machines were kept locked, and one had to apply for permission to own a typewriter—and I wondered how *Pravda*, formerly the official mouthpiece of the Communist Party, was coping with all the changes. President Gorbachev edged away from rigid Marxism after the Party betrayed him. But *Pravda* had brazenly supported the August coup. Shut down by Boris Yeltsin as punishment for that treachery, the newspaper had only recently resumed publication.

Pravda has a fabled history. Founded in 1912, it predates the Revolution, and enlarged photos in its office lobby show Lenin personally poring over typesetting galleys. Everyone knew the paper used to present as much propaganda as news. (Russians enjoyed this play on words about their two largest newspapers, *Pravda*, meaning "Truth," and *Izvestiya*, meaning "News": "There is no 'pravda' in *Izvestiya* and no 'izvestiya' in *Pravda*.") Still, reading *Pravda* was compulsory for any citizen of note. Many careers and even lives have been determined by a few sentences in *Pravda*.

The newspaper occupied a large, five-story building in the heart of Moscow's printing district, but many offices in that building now sat vacant. Numbers tell the dramatic story of *Pravda*'s fall from grace: daily circulation had plummeted from eleven million to 700,000. *Pravda* had cut four-fifths of its foreign correspondents and reduced its overall staff by two-thirds. It was losing money on every subscription, and scrambled to obtain enough paper to stay in print.

The editor in chief, accompanied by several senior editors, met with us in a rather bare, functional conference room used mainly for editorial planning meetings. He spoke for about fifteen minutes, detailing the "challenges" facing his paper, and then turned the meeting over to a younger editor, a senior correspondent who would soon move to Washington, DC and head up the US bureau.

Like an optimistic surgeon discussing a stage four cancer patient, the editor in chief tried to put the best face on *Pravda*'s crisis even while admitting the prognosis looked grim. It soon became apparent why our delegation had been invited to these offices: we got the unsettling feeling of being used in a kind of reverse propaganda. The official organ of the Communist Party, utterly discredited, was in an act of desperation reaching out to its antithesis—evangelical Christianity—as a way of gaining credibility, or at least gaining sales.

What about reprinting from the Bible? one of our group asked. Excellent idea, said the editors. We welcome reprints from your "holy books." How about a column on religion? Splendid! Can you suggest a writer?

The editors sought to rehabilitate *Pravda*'s image by taking the moral high ground. "The most important principle to us is reconciliation," they told us. "We strive to bring our people together. The past months have shown that our level of civilization is still low. We don't know how to settle disputes in a civilized, peaceful way. We must find a way to reform our people from the inside. We must learn to settle differences by civilized—one could even say Christian—means."

Conversation turned to the question of how one comes up with the moral principles worth advocating. Early Communists believed that they—not God—were the ones to determine morality, which could then be enforced from the top down. The history of communism proves beyond all doubt that goodness cannot be legislated from the Kremlin and enforced at the point of a gun. In a great irony, attempts to compel morality tend to produce rebellious subjects and tyrannical rulers.

As the quintessential propaganda vehicle, *Pravda* had, after all, always taken a moral stance; the problem was that the moral principles shifted depending on who was in power. Currently *Pravda* was showing admirable compassion for the victims of the Chernobyl disaster; they gave us sample drawings by the children of Chernobyl that they were using as a fundraiser. But the same newspaper had, for example, shown no compassion whatever for the children who died during Stalin's enforced starvation of Ukraine. What "higher law" determined when compassion applied and when it did not?

Pravda had no answer. The editors readily acknowledged that their nation was facing perhaps the greatest crisis in its history, and they agreed about the nature of that crisis. We cited what a prominent government economist had told us: "The worst crisis these days is morality. Ideology, which was a religion for us, has been crushed. Yet there is no Christ to replace it." These seemed to us surprising words from a businessman devoted to improving the material state of the country, but the *Pravda* editors concurred. "Yes, he's right. It's the worst crisis, worse than the economic and political problems."

Listening to the editors gathered around the table, I could easily sense their inner tumult. They had risen through the ranks because of their staunch loyalty to Marxist doctrine—some had still not renounced their Party membership—and yet they now knew the ideology had failed miserably. What could replace it? I thought of an ironic term from chemistry, "free radicals": these editors were looking for some particle of reality to attach themselves to.

Unaccountably, I found myself feeling something like pity for the editors. They were not the horned demons I had envisioned in high school.

They were earnest, sincere, searching—and badly shaken. Shaken to the foundations. They clung, as if by their fingernails, to the original vision of justice and equality espoused by Marx and Lenin. Yet even while clinging, they admitted the pursuit of that vision had produced the worst nightmares the world has ever seen.

I tried to put myself in their place. I, too, am an editor committed to an ideology. I, too, have sat around a conference table and discussed the best way to present a vision of truth to my readers. What must it be like to get dressed every morning and come to work knowing that the vast majority of my former readers have repudiated everything I have always believed, but not knowing what else to believe?

Reflecting back on the meeting with *Pravda*, Martin DeHaan of the Radio Bible Class drew the direct analogy to us. "How would we evangelicals feel," he said, "if our Christian faith were exposed as a fraud—if we learned that Christ had not risen after all?" The apostle Paul toyed with that hypothetical question. "And if Christ has not been raised, our preaching is useless and so is your faith," he thundered in 1 Corinthians 15; "More than that, we are then found to be false witnesses . . . we are to be pitied more than all men." Down deep, at the core, all of us would be shattered. We would know that the center of our faith, that upon which we had built our lives and invested all our hopes, had been destroyed. A corpse cannot be the Lord of Creation.

I sensed in these communist editors something like that upheaval. Early communists had promised the emergence of a new breed of human being, the "New Socialist Man," who would demonstrate superior noble character. Leon Trotsky wrote in 1924, "Man will become immeasurably stronger, wiser and subtler; his body will become more harmonized, his movements more rhythmic, his voice more musical. The forms of life will become dynamically dramatic. The average human type will rise to the heights of an Aristotle, a Goethe or a Marx. And above this ridge new peaks will rise."

In light of the Soviet Union's history of violence, imminent threats of civil war, a failed coup, and an economy in shambles, such words seemed mocking. Today, any Russian would laugh out loud at Trotsky's prediction. The *Pravda* editors were shaken to the core, so much so that they were now meeting with nineteen emissaries of a religion their founder had scorned as "the opiate of the people," asking us for help. "Christian values may be the only thing to keep our country from falling apart," said the editor in chief of *Pravda*.

I recalled an article I had read in *The Atlantic Monthly* in 1989. "Can We Be Good Without God?" asked Glenn Tinder in the cover story, echoing the famous line from Dostoevsky. Tinder's conclusion was, No. Apart from a higher moral code before which every political leader, no matter how powerful, must bow, and apart from an infusion of love that transmutes human selfishness into Christian charity and selflessness, a society will gradually but inevitably tilt toward chaos on the one hand or tyranny on the other. The Soviet Union, which had tried harder than any other nation to be "good" without God, had had its fill of tyranny. Now, what would keep it from chaos?

The editors of *Pravda* remarked wistfully that Christianity and communism have many of the same ideals. Some have even called communism a "Christian heresy" because of its emphasis on equality, sharing, justice, and racial harmony. But "seventy-four years on the road to nowhere," which is how Russians derisively refer to their Marxist past, have taught that the grandest social experiment in human history was terribly flawed.

Classical Marxists preached atheism and fought fiercely against religion for a shrewd reason: In order to inspire workers to rise up violently against their oppressors, Marxists had to kill off any hope in a heavenly life beyond this one, and any fear of divine punishment.

A Romanian pastor named Josif Ton once wrote of the contradiction that lies at the heart of a Marxist view of humanity. "[They teach] their pupils that life is the product of chance combinations of matter, that it is governed by Darwinian laws of adaptation and survival, and that it is man's only chance. There is no after-life, no 'savior' to reward self-sacrifice or to punish egoism or rapacity. After the pupils have been thus taught, I am sent in to teach them to be noble and honorable men and women, expending all their energies on doing good for the benefit of society, even to the point of self-sacrifice. They must be courteous, tell only the truth, and live a morally pure life. But they lack motivation for goodness. They see that in a purely material world only he who hurries and grabs for himself possesses anything. Why should they be self-denying and honest? What motive can be offered them to live lives of usefulness to others?"

The *Pravda* editors conceded that they were having a hard time motivating people to show compassion. The average Soviet citizen would rather spend his money on drink than support needy children. A recent poll had revealed that 70 percent of Russian parents would not allow their children to have contact with a disabled child; 80 percent would not give money to help; some advocated infanticide.

Early experiments in capitalism were not going well either, because salespeople were surly and disinterested. The whole country seemed in a state of depression and despair. "How do you reform, change, motivate people?" the editors asked us.

Humans dream of systems so perfect that no one will need to be good, wrote T. S. Eliot, who saw many of his friends embrace the dream of Marxism. "But the man that is will shadow the man that pretends to be." What we were hearing from Soviet leaders, and the KGB, and now *Pravda*, was that the Soviet Union ended up with the worst of both: a society far from perfect, and a people who had forgotten how to be good.

I am perplexed by my own data and my conclusion is a direct contradiction of the original idea with which I start. Starting from unlimited freedom, I arrive at unlimited despotism. I will add, however, that there can be no solution of the social problem but mine.

—FYODOR DOSTOEVSKY
THE POSSESSED

CHAPTER 10

The Last Marxist in Moscow

THE DAY AFTER OUR meeting with a subdued *Pravda*, a direct and challenging confrontation with Marxist ideology finally came our way, on a visit to the Academy of Social Sciences. The name is misleading: until the August coup the academy functioned as the preeminent finishing school for Marxist-Leninist leaders. Raisa Gorbachev once taught there, and many world leaders from the former socialist bloc have studied at this elite school.

Like everything else in Russia, the academy is undergoing tumultuous change. Until the fall of 1991 it received generous funding from the Communist Party, but shortly before our visit subsidies were abruptly cut off. The academy's professors, once coddled and privileged, now literally had no idea where their next paychecks would come from.

I had grown accustomed to the shabby look of most Moscow buildings. Pre-revolutionary buildings retained a certain charm, but most had peeling paint and wallpaper. Modern buildings, such as the one that housed *Pravda*, looked like winners in a "Design the ugliest building!" contest.

Inside most government buildings, long dim hallways connected a warren of cubbyhole offices, each furnished with standard-issue desks and chairs. The Academy of Social Sciences, in sharp contrast, looked as if it had been helicoptered in intact from Scandinavia. Former United Nations ambassador Jeane Kirkpatrick on a recent visit had commented, "It's the only place I saw in Russia that looked like it had a landlord."

How could such luxury be lavished on a university? I wondered as our bus pulled into the towering marble complex. The hall we visited reminded me of the Kennedy Center in Washington, DC. Enormous crystal chandeliers hung from a forty-foot ceiling, giving off enough candlepower to light the Moscow Airport several times over. An enclosed courtyard with a fountain and tropical plants dominated the foyer, designed so that the eye moved immediately to an imposing statue of Lenin carved out of gleaming white stone. A freestanding marble staircase curved up toward plush offices and meeting rooms.

Gawking like tourists, we climbed the marble stairway to the auditorium where academy professors awaited us. The auditorium also had chandeliers; its walls were covered partly with wood paneling and partly with gilded wallpaper that would have looked more appropriate in the Palace of Versailles. Conference tables made of dark tropical woods formed a long U-shape, and fifty professors were assembled around the tables. Each place at the table was wired for simultaneous translation in several languages, and state-of-the-art video cameras mounted on the walls recorded the event for posterity.

Much like *Pravda*, the Academy of Social Sciences in its scramble to survive was reaching out to Christians, who still had some credibility with a restive populace. A parade of notables from American Christendom had recently visited, and the academy was negotiating to establish a department for the study of Christianity.

As the dialogue with academy professors proceeded, I sensed the same confusion we had seen in the *Pravda* editors. Of all people in the Soviet Union, these professors were true believers. Fed communist theory practically from birth, they had devoted their lives to the propagation of it. One could still see relics of that intense devotion in the quasi-religious signs posted around Russia: "Lenin Lived. Lenin Lives. Lenin Will Live."

The professors recognized they had lost, perhaps forever, the battle of ideas. The cherished Marxist dream was over. They wanted to appear open to new ideas, such as capitalism and a free press, but the changes they had

seen so far hardly seemed like improvements. In Moscow capitalism flourished mainly on Arbat Street, where teenagers employed by the Russian
mafia exploited foreign tourists, the only people with hard currency. The
soft-core porn magazines springing up—*Playboy* had just inaugurated a
Russian edition—as well as American television programs now available by
satellite chilled them. Their daughters were talking about becoming hard-
currency hookers, their sons were scheming for profits on the black market.
Where was the ethics in this new freedom? they asked us.

Freedom scared them, and yet they could not deny its benefits. One
academy historian, borrowing from Tocqueville, mentioned the two
streams that can issue from a common source of revolution: one leads to
free arrangements among citizens, the other leads to absolute power.

"We started with common ideals," he said. "Leaders of both our societies talked about justice and equality and individual rights. Yet somehow
you have produced a society that with all its problems still conveys courtesy
and civility. I have been to the United States, and I see the difference even in
the faces of your shopkeepers. Your minorities protest against discrimina-
tion—but they do not secede or start civil wars.

"Somehow, beginning from similar ideals, we have produced a society
of beasts. We have murdered our own citizens in the name of the state.
We know that we must move toward liberal democracy, but we don't know
how. We no longer know what values to build a society upon."

Most groups in Moscow plied us eagerly with questions. The academy
professors seemed more anxious to talk. Listening to them, I felt I was in
a political therapy session, nodding my head sympathetically as neurotic
clients let long-suppressed anxieties spill out. It felt good to be listening for
a change, after all the talking we had done.

In the midst of this genteel discussion, one of the Marxist professors,
a specialist in philosophy, rose to his feet and asked for the floor (all other
speakers had remained seated). Blotches of red appeared on his face, and as
soon as he began speaking anger gushed forth. Others in the room looked
around anxiously, concerned that he was straying from the mannerly
dialogue. But there was no stopping this man. He had come to deliver a
speech—a diatribe, really—not to fraternize with the enemy.

The academy translator valiantly struggled to keep pace for a while,
then waved for the professor to slow down, and finally gave up entirely.
Russian speakers in our group did their best to fill in, but the philosopher
never paused to allow them to catch up.

We managed to catch enough words to grasp the essence of his argument. "We need not have God to have morality!" he said. "Erich Fromm developed a fine morality based on Man with a capital 'M.' God is not necessary. Why pretend there is a God?"

The philosopher's volume rose and his face grew even more flushed. He punctuated the air with his finger as he made each point, and I thought of the paintings of Lenin addressing the workers. I thought too of stump preachers in the South where I had grown up. Of course! This man was a fanatic evangelist, the last true-blue, dyed-in-the-wool Marxist in Moscow. He was out to gain converts, and it mattered not at all if he was the last person in the world to believe these things. He was a bitter, wounded atheist, and he seized the chance to strike back.

"Marxism has not failed!" he shouted. "Yes, Stalin made mistakes. Yes, even our beloved Lenin made mistakes. Perhaps even Marx made mistakes. But go back to the young Marx, not the old Marx. There you will find the purity of the socialist vision. There you will find a morality based on Man with the capital 'M.' That is what we need. As for Christianity, we already tried that in Russia—for one thousand years we tried it."

We members of Christian Bridge were fidgeting in our seats. Being yelled at by a fanatic is not a pleasant sensation, I realized, and tucked away the thought for further reflection. I whispered to the person next to me, "The problem with the young Marx is that he keeps turning into the old Marx." A few other members of our group were whispering to their seatmates, and still others were clearing their throats, ready to jump in with a rebuttal.

The philosopher went on for ten or fifteen minutes until finally the emcee forced him to stop. I sensed in the atmosphere of the room an odd mixture of revenge and embarrassment. The professors waited for our response, and I cringed at the possibilities. Some of us weren't far removed from stump preachers ourselves, I knew, and the last thing the academy needed was a wounded evangelical doing battle with a wounded atheist. By the providence of God, it was Kent Hill, director of the Institute on Religion and Democracy (IRD), who got the floor.

Kent Hill looks more professorial than the professors. He wears glasses, has a scholarly demeanor, and speaks in soft, measured tones, the epitome of rational discourse. He also has a PhD in Russian studies and was a Fulbright scholar in Moscow before taking the position at IRD. I did not envy him the spotlight he had just stepped into, but I could not imagine a finer representative to respond on our behalf.

"First, I want to affirm your right to your beliefs," Kent began, and waited respectfully for the translator to plug in his microphone and resume his work. "I am concerned about intolerance in the Soviet Union today—intolerance of atheists. I recently learned of an incident where a group allowed a Christian believer to speak, but shouted down an atheist. We have not come in that spirit. We support freedom of religion, and that includes freedom for those who do not believe in God."

Tension rushed from the room as if someone had opened an air lock. The professors nodded approval, and even the philosopher gave a curt nod. Kent continued.

"The issues you have raised tonight, sir, are important issues. In fact, I cannot think of more important issues to discuss. You have touched on questions of ultimate meaning for humanity and for the universe. Our group has thought long and hard about these questions. We have reached some conclusions, and we would love to discuss those with you.

"But one night's discussion would hardly do justice to these issues. I do not feel comfortable presenting a brief response. Could I make a suggestion? My family and I are moving to Moscow in December, and I will be teaching a course in Christian apologetics at Moscow State University. I will gladly return to your academy with Christian friends and set up a forum in which we can consider these important matters."

Again, nods of approval all around. Kent resumed, "But since I have the floor, I would like to mention why I believe the way I do." At this point, Kent lapsed into fluent Russian. The professors, some with looks of astonishment on their faces, removed their headphones and now we English speakers were the ones listening to the simultaneous translation.

Kent told of a time of doubt in his life when he was tempted to abandon his Christian beliefs. He began reading Dostoevsky's great novel *The Brothers Karamazov*—at this mention, more nods—which deals with many of the issues raised by the academy philosopher.

"At first I found myself attracted to Ivan, the agnostic. His arguments against God were powerful, especially those concerning the problem of evil. I sensed in him a sincerity and a brilliant mind. As I read Dostoevsky's book, I found myself gradually losing faith. But to my surprise, I was eventually won over by the love shown by Ivan's brother Alyosha. Ivan had fine arguments, but he had no love. He could reason his way to a morality, but he could not create the love necessary to fulfill it. Eventually, I came to believe in Christ because I found in him a source for that love."

With that, Kent Hill sat down, and our meeting with the Academy of Social Sciences was transformed.

It occurred to me as we drove away from the ghostly marble buildings that Kent Hill had done far more than defuse one awkward confrontation. He had given us a model of evangelism for the shattered Soviet empire, perhaps the only model that will authentically work. First, he had begun with a genuine respect for the Soviets' own beliefs, even those diametrically opposed to his own. Unlike the philosophy professor, he had listened with courtesy and compassion before speaking.

Next, by moving to Moscow, Kent had committed himself to incarnational ministry. By themselves, no delegations of foreigners visiting for a week or a month will bring long-term change to the country. But a sprinkling of dedicated people who share the hardships and the turmoil, people willing to stand shoulder-to-shoulder in the Moscow bread lines, could perhaps become the salt that savors the whole society.

Finally, Kent pointed to the source of truth latent in the Russian culture itself. His lapse into the Russian language, almost instinctive as his response turned personal, and his reference to Dostoevsky communicated far more to that audience than if he had quoted an entire epistle from the New Testament.

It was through reading Dostoevsky that Solzhenitsyn first began to understand the primacy of the spiritual over the material, a revelation that ultimately led to his conversion in a labor camp. Then Solzhenitsyn, too, became a directional signal pointing the way back toward God. As Kent Hill had so gently revealed, the seeds of renewal already lay in Russian soil.

What has happened with us? Who and for which transgressions has plunged us into this abyss of evil and misfortunes? Who has extinguished the light of virtue in our souls . . . the sacred light of our consciousness? We used to live with light in our souls . . . without scratching out the eyes of our neighbors, without breaking our neighbor's bones. Why has all this been abducted from us, and replaced by godlessness? . . . To whom are we going to turn our prayers now . . . to ask forgiveness?

—VIKTOR ASTAFYEV
"PLACE OF ACTION"

CHAPTER 11

Awakenings

IN HIS BOOK *AWAKENINGS*, Dr. Oliver Sacks relates the case histories of twenty patients who lived in a suspended state of motionlessness and lowered metabolism brought about by a "sleeping sickness," encephalitis. Sacks discovered that the drug L-DOPA had a remarkable effect on such patients. A woman named Rose, semiconscious for forty-three years, came to life, began moving her arms and legs, talked, and resumed contact with the world around her.

Everyone reacted to the drug a little differently, though. A few people realized an almost total cure, and were able to recommence a normal life. Others, like Leonard (the character played by Robert DeNiro in the 1990 movie version) experienced a brief and dramatic remission that ended when their bodies proved intolerant of L-DOPA. They had a few weeks of conversation, of walking outdoors, of dancing in the moonlight, before they lapsed again into a "frozen," immobile state.

In a case study published elsewhere, Sacks tells of a third response. Uncle Toby had sat silent in a corridor for seven years, his metabolic rate reduced to near zero. His body temperature hovered around thirty degrees below normal, yet with food and water he somehow stayed alive: "alive, but not alive; in abeyance, in cold storage," as Dr. Sacks puts it. After a month's treatment with a thyroid drug, Uncle Toby awakened. Amazingly, he could walk and talk, although he had no memory of the previous seven years. Doctors, Uncle Toby's family, and Uncle Toby himself rejoiced at this Lazarus-like miracle. But something else awakened too: a highly malignant carcinoma in Uncle Toby's chest, inactive for the past seven years, unexpectedly sprang to life. Uncle Toby died, in a fit of coughing, a few days after his awakening.

Which direction will the Soviet Union—even the term is anachronistic now—go? On my 1991 visit, I saw signs of awakening everywhere. Vendors sold merchandise openly on Arbat Street; Pizza Hut, McDonald's, and other franchises were moving in; the government was reconverting seven thousand ancient churches, used as garages and warehouses, into places of worship. Muscovites danced in the moonlight. How long would the dance last? Was it only a brief remission before the disease broke loose again?

Russia does not have an encouraging history. "Tyranny is a habit which may be developed until at last it becomes a disease," wrote Dostoevsky. A century later Solzhenitsyn added, "Left to ourselves, with only the help of the spherical object pivoted on the neckbone, we are more likely than not to take the wrong road." Whatever a people will submit to, a tyrant will arise to exploit, and Russia has a long pattern of submission. Some muttered darkly that Boris Yeltsin was such a tyrant: a throwback to the past, a malignancy unfrozen by a three-day August awakening.

Mass confusion reigns, as reflected daily in news stories from Moscow. Our last night there, our own delegation got a small taste of the kind of turmoil that prevails. We were staying in a splendid hotel that had formerly belonged to the Central Committee. When the Communist Party was disgraced after the coup, the state government took over such properties—or so it thought. Upon checking into the hotel, we received identity cards marked "Guests of the President," and got assurances that the government would pick up the cost of our rooms. But when the time came to pay the bill, the hotel demanded hard currency.

Several times over the next few days we witnessed the bizarre scene of a personal aide to President Gorbachev arguing with the hotel manager over who owned the fourteen-story structure. "It's our hotel, it belongs to the government!" the aide contended. "Fine, then pay the bill with government funds. But we only accept hard currency," the manager shot back, unyielding.

The night of our departure, this argument went on for four hours, finally ending at 2 AM in a compromise. The hotel agreed to accept two-thirds of the payment in rubles, but demanded one-third in hard currency. Gorbachev's government had no dollars even to issue its own ambassadors, and the humiliated aide had no choice but to turn to us for help. Fortunately, some of the veterans in our group, anticipating just such a problem, had brought along a large amount of cash. They knocked on doors in the middle of the night and collected the remainder of what was needed—seven thousand dollars—so that we could depart the hotel.

Similar scenarios play out a thousand times each day. Who owns any building? For more than seventy years there has been no such thing as "private property" there. In a literal sense, the whole country is up for grabs.

In *Crime and Punishment* Dostoevsky writes of the perilous sensation of living on one square yard of a cliff, on a narrow ledge where two feet can hardly stand, surrounded on all sides by an abyss, the ocean, everlasting darkness, everlasting solitude, and an everlasting storm. A good image for Russia and its neighbors, I decided. Everyone knows the danger on all sides; no one knows how to get off the cliff. Soon, very soon, the nation will have to step off the one square yard of cliff.

The day after the hotel fiasco our Lufthansa jet took off, lifting above the cloud cover, and I had my final glimpse of Russia. Already I was feeling the shock of reentry: I caught myself staring at the warm, expressive face of the flight attendant—a German at that—as she smilingly interacted with the passengers, distributing blankets, pillows, and headphones with a combination of professionalism and courtesy such as I had not seen since entering the country.

I arrived back in the US on the seventy-fourth anniversary of the Bolshevik takeover, an event that has defined much of the history of the twentieth century. Television news reported that for the first time no official parades were held in Moscow. Later that week Boris Yeltsin banned most Communist Party activities from Russian soil, thereby writing what may be the final chapter of the grand experiment.

What went wrong? Every day the news media report symptoms of a fatally flawed economic system. Curiously, I have not seen one mention in the media of what every Soviet leader insisted to us: the gravest crisis is not economic or political, but rather moral and spiritual. The failure of Marxism, we were told again and again, is above all a *theological* failure.

In his Templeton Address in 1983, Aleksandr Solzhenitsyn said,

> Over half a century ago, while I was still a child, I recall hearing a number of older people offer the following explanation for the great disasters that had befallen Russia: "Men have forgotten God; that's why all this has happened." Since then I have spent well-nigh fifty years working on the history of our revolution; in the process I have read hundreds of books, collected hundreds of personal testimonies, and have already contributed eight volumes of my own toward the effort of clearing away the rubble left by that upheaval. But if I were asked today to formulate as concisely as possible the main cause of the ruinous revolution that swallowed up some sixty million of our people, I could not put it more accurately than to repeat: "Men have forgotten God; that's why all this has happened."

Solzhenitsyn went on to say, "I myself see Christianity today as the only living spiritual force capable of undertaking the spiritual healing of Russia." When he made those remarks, the USSR was still a superpower and Solzhenitsyn was widely assailed for his old-fashioned views. Now, less than a decade later our delegation heard almost the identical assessment from top leaders of the nation. Above any other nation, the Soviet Union endeavored to get along without God. "Religion will disappear," Marx flatly predicted, its quaint beliefs made obsolete by the New Socialist Man. But religion did not disappear, and no New Socialist Man emerged.

In this century a morality play has been conducted on grand scale, with catastrophic consequences. What lies ahead? On the airplane on the way home, various members of Project Christian Bridge tried to speculate. We all sensed the enormity of change that has already come. The new openness toward religion exceeded what any of us might have hoped for. In that regard, the prayers of millions of Christians inside and outside Russia have been answered.

Joel Nederhood, a member of our delegation, had this response: "Very few times in life do you get to sense the epic, the magnificent work of God. I believe that in our week together we experienced the epic. We saw a foretaste of Philippians 2, 'At the name of Jesus every knee shall bow.' God is doing something magnificent in Russia."

I, too, sensed the epic, and yet I confess that I tend toward realism, and hope does not come easily for me. I can hardly envision what a reconstituted, much less a redeemed, Soviet Union would look like.

One thing only gives me hope. I will never forget the expressions on the faces of Basil, and the teenage prisoners in Zagorsk, and the female television newscaster, and even the vice chairman of the KGB. Jesus' parables about the kingdom and the fig tree and the great banquet make one truth explicit: God goes where he is wanted. God does not force himself on an individual or on a nation, whether it be first-century Jews or twenty-first-century Americans. And as I look back on my visit to Russia, one impression lingers above all others: never in my life have I been among people with a more ravenous appetite for God.

Left, above: **Konstantin Lubenchenko**, newly elected chairman of the Supreme Soviet, told us, "We need Bibles here very much. Is there a way to distribute them free of charge so more people can get them?"

Right: After a prayer, **Mikhail Morgulis** presented a Bible to **General Nikolai Stolyarov**, second in command of the KGB.

Left: "There were many years when I had no encouragement. And now, such changes, I can hardly believe them," **Basil** said in closing.

Below: **Alex Leonovich** epitomizes the old guard of warriors who have prayed for more than half a century that change might come to Russia.

Top: Zagorsk is a feast for the eyes, a veritable Disneyland of sacred architecture.

Center, left: "We are in a crisis, a spiritual crisis," **Mikhail Gorbachev** said. ". . . More than ever before, we need support from our partners, and I value solidarity with religion."

Top: After meeting with the delegation, **Gorbachev** shook hands with each member. Here he is greeting **Peter** and **Anita Deyneka,** while **Philip Yancey** and **John Van Diest** look on.

Above: Signs of awakening were everywhere. Vendors sold merchandise openly on Arbat Street. . . . Muscovites danced in the streets. How long will the dance last?

PART THREE

Russia's U-Turn
and Ukraine's Rebirth

by Philip Yancey and John A. Bernbaum

CHAPTER 12

The Light That Dimmed

WE LEFT RUSSIA CONVINCED that our delegation had witnessed an earth-shaking revolution. It had begun in 1989, when the hated Berlin Wall fell without a shot being fired. Next, the world looked on with astonishment as countries such as Czechoslovakia, Hungary, Poland, and Romania shed the shackles of communism. Soon client states within the USSR likewise declared their independence until, shortly after our 1991 visit, the super-power known as the Soviet Union ceased to exist. President George H. W. Bush would announce the official end of the Cold War on Christmas Day, 1991.

A few days after my return from Russia, I [Philip Yancey] gave a report on Christian Bridge before a standing-room-only crowd at my church, recounting our meetings with Mikhail Gorbachev, the Supreme Soviet, *Pravda*, the Academy of Social Sciences, the Journalists' Club, and the KGB. I held up the *Matryoshka* doll I had purchased from a street vendor. After some debate I had chosen one with Gorbachev, not Boris Yeltsin, as the outermost figure, for he was the one orchestrating the revolution.

Robert G. Kaiser, a *Washington Post* correspondent stationed in Moscow, described the shocking metamorphosis: "In just over five years, Mikhail Gorbachev transformed the world. He turned his own country upside down. He woke a sleeping giant, the people of the Soviet Union, and gave them freedoms they had never dreamed of. He tossed away the Soviet Empire; he ended the Cold War. These are the most astounding historical developments that any of us are likely to experience."

A few weeks later I visited my ninety-three-year-old grandmother in Philadelphia. She listened attentively as I described the dramatic changes taking place in Russia. "Grandmother, Russia's a different place now," I said, "no longer our enemy, and no longer an atheist state." I told her about jogging through a Moscow park, where I came across huge statues of Stalin, Marx, Lenin, and other Communist heroes lying in a snowy field. They had been toppled from their pedestals and deposited in a kind of dumping ground. Russia's gods had failed them, and the nation was now searching for a new god.

She stroked her chin, and I could hear her dentures clicking as she absorbed what I was saying. Finally, she spoke. "I remember when those boys took over," she said, and it took me a minute to realize she was speaking of the Bolsheviks in 1917. "I didn't think it would last." Born in 1898, my grandmother had outlived the grand experiment of Russian communism.

I have already mentioned the effect of growing up during the Cold War, when schools scheduled "duck and cover" exercises to teach us how to respond if the Soviet Union someday launched its arsenal of nuclear weapons against the United States. Over the years I read scores of books on Soviet communism, including Solzhenitsyn's devastating critiques. I also read the major novels and short stories by Tolstoy and Dostoevsky, which helped to shape my Christian faith. I returned from Russia in 1991 stunned and bewildered by what I had seen and heard. Could it be possible that atheistic Russia would now rediscover the spiritual roots it had tried so fervidly to sever?

Fast forward three decades, however, and it appears that Russia has made an abrupt U-turn and now moves in the opposite direction. A democracy in name only, the nation in the twenty-first century has been led by an autocrat intent on reversing course. In 2022 President Vladimir Putin, who once called the collapse of the Soviet empire "the greatest geopolitical catastrophe of the [twentieth] century," launched a war against Ukraine with the intent to forcibly regain territory. In every way—economically, politically, spiritually—Russia has clamped down on freedom and turned away from the West, which it now views as a hostile threat.

In his book *Perestroika*, Gorbachev had set out the nation's urgent need: "Today our main job is to lift the individual spiritually, respecting his inner world and giving him moral strength and help." For a time, Russia opened wide the window. Gorbachev had, after all, personally invited the Christian Bridge delegation. During the next few years, thousands of missionaries would respond to his appeal for spiritual help. Yet as quickly as it opened, the window began to close in the 1990s and slammed shut when Vladimir Putin became Russia's president.

In future years, historians will sort through the various reasons for the nation's about-face. As I listen to the news reports from Russia now—fleeing émigrés, assassinations, mass arrests, press clampdowns, war crimes, nuclear threats—I keep replaying the gripping scenes I witnessed in 1991: dazed *Pravda* editors grasping for truth, peasants standing in a packed chapel in Zagorsk, journalists applauding prisoners, and even KGB agents issuing a public apology. It seemed as if an entire ideology was melting around me. Instead it went underground, only to reappear in a more sinister form.

What went wrong, both politically and spiritually? For help in answering that question, I have turned to one of the nineteen "Guests of the President" on our 1991 visit, my friend John Bernbaum. After earning a PhD in European and Russian history, John served with the US Department of State until joining the Christian College Coalition, where he developed a Russian studies program. In 1990 he accepted the invitation of Russia's Minister of Science and Education to establish a Christian liberal arts college in Moscow.

For three decades John commuted back and forth between Moscow, Kyiv, and Washington, DC—more than 110 trips in all. The Russian-American Christian University, which John founded and led, stayed open for fifteen years, until the U-turn engineered by Putin. During those years, John witnessed firsthand the thawing, then freezing, between Russia and the West as he dealt with government bureaucrats, contractors, and students. The rest of this book relies heavily on John's observations and insights.

As he reflects, "I believed that Russia needed a foundation to fill the moral vacuum, one that integrated faith with such fields as science, the humanities, psychology, history, politics, and business. I told an inquiring journalist as I moved to Moscow, 'This is truly one of those rare moments of truth in a nation's history when basic decisions are being made that will set the future course for millions of people.' Little did I know that I would live through such a series of tumultuous events, with such an unexpected outcome."

CHAPTER 13

After the Fall

MIKHAIL GORBACHEV, WHO CAME to power in 1985, had an immense impact on history by making radical changes in the Soviet Union and building friendly relationships with US presidents. We knew about his economic and political reforms and his desire to wind down the Cold War, but few of us realized the dramatic spiritual dynamics that were also astir.

When I [John Bernbaum] was invited to bring a delegation of Christian educators to the Soviet Union in October 1990 to discuss educational exchanges with Russian universities, I had no idea what to expect. I assumed that the decades of anti-American propaganda would make these discussions a challenge. Instead, our group was overwhelmed by the warm welcome we received.

Shortly after arriving in Moscow, we were divided into small groups and assigned to different state universities in cities across the Soviet Union. My group of three went to Gorky (renamed Nizhny Novgorod two days before we arrived), which had been off-limits to foreigners since the 1930s because of its military industries. Our trip by overnight train was my first of many, which I thoroughly enjoyed—apart from the problem of too little sleep.

Near the end of our three-day visit to Nizhny Novgorod State University (NNSU), I was asked with little advance warning to speak to university students and faculty. To my great surprise, I was ushered into a packed auditorium. I made some comments about Christian higher education and the possibility of exchange programs between NNSU and Christian universities in the States, and then responded to questions from the students.

After these stimulating exchanges with students, the university's president told us that the students wanted to share some music with us. Four students with guitars sang several songs in English, including a rousing rendition of "When the Saints Go Marching In," and "Ain't Gonna Study War No More." Then followed the Gorky Academic Choir, comprising forty formally dressed men and women, who gave a brief concert: a song of praise from the Russian Orthodox liturgy, another American spiritual, "Who's Knocking at the Door?," and the classic "Song of the Volga Boatmen."

I could not believe what I was hearing in this, my first introduction to the spiritual revival underway. Russian students from isolated Nizhny Novgorod, who had never met Americans, were singing in excellent English about Jesus knocking on the door of their hearts. We knew nothing about this emerging spiritual interest that followed seven decades of atheism and the brutal persecution of Christians and other religious groups.

The Christian Bridge trip to Moscow a year later (described in Part Two) revealed that Soviet government leaders and intellectual elites shared the same desire to learn more about the Christian faith. Soon, however, many of the leaders we met were removed by the populist politician Boris Yeltsin, who edged Gorbachev to the sidelines. Priorities changed, and Soviet societies began to fragment.

When Gorbachev introduced the openness of *perestroika*, he was focusing on economic restructuring and did not anticipate the fervor for freedom in Soviet republics such as Estonia, Latvia, Ukraine, and Georgia. His successor Yeltsin seemed content to let the Soviet Union unravel, and all but two of its fifteen republics quickly declared their independence. Observers joked that the Union of Soviet Socialist Republics (USSR) was becoming the Union of Fewer and Fewer Republics (UFFR).

Change swept through the continent at a breathtaking pace. With the breakup of the USSR and the dismantling of Soviet control in Eastern Europe, almost thirty nations were born or reconstituted. Dictators were overthrown in favor of elected leaders, and a newly energized free press sprang up throughout the former Soviet Union.

As the dust settled, Yeltsin emerged as the real winner, elected president of the Russian Federation. Despite shedding its empire, Russia remained the largest country on earth, nearly twice the size of the United States. With the Cold War over, political consultants from the West poured into Russia and its former satellites with visions of a new era of global cooperation.

It was a time of buoyant hope, especially for Christians eager to support their fellow believers who had suffered so much persecution since 1917. The collapse of Communism and disbanding of the Soviet Union opened up unprecedented opportunities. Early on, Campus Crusade for Christ (now CRU) gained permission to show its "Jesus Film" in the Soviet Union. Soon education officials from formerly communist countries and republics requested that the film be shown in their public schools. Many of these officials also invited the Jesus Film Project staff to train schoolteachers in Christian ethics.

Soviet teachers were echoing what we had heard from government leaders about a spiritual vacuum, and appealed for help. As one teacher remarked, "It is very hard to live without believing in anything." A survey found that only 25 percent of Russian teachers ranked the economy as the most serious problem; rather, educators stressed the need for a new moral foundation. Some cited Solzhenitsyn, who named Christianity as the only spiritual force capable of healing Russia. Given the nation's history of religious repression, no one could have imagined such a turnabout.

Within a year of our Christian Bridge trip, eighty-two Christian organizations cooperated to form the CoMission, the largest mission partnership in history. In November 1992, the Russian Ministry of Education and the CoMission agreed on a five-year partnership to develop morals and ethics programs for public schools. Some 1,500 American volunteers raised funds and moved to Russia in order to train teachers. Forgoing modern conveniences, they lived in tiny apartments where hot water and a working elevator were luxuries. Over the next six years, these volunteers trained more than 42,000 formerly Communist educators to teach a Christian ethics curriculum in the public schools.

By 1996, some five thousand Western and South Korean missionaries were working in the former Soviet Union. Not surprisingly, the new atmosphere of freedom attracted cults as well as sincere but naive emissaries who had little sensitivity to Russian culture. Nonetheless, several Christian universities were established, as well as a number of Bible institutes and colleges.

The explosion of Christian education and the training of Russian schoolteachers came as a shock—and, to some, an unwanted foreign intrusion—in a nation that had once tried to eradicate religion. Yet the resurgence of religion in the former USSR received little press coverage and almost no attention from Western officials and policy analysts.

∂❧

Jack Matlock Jr., the American ambassador to Russia from 1987 to 1991, compared the complexity of transitioning from communism toward democracy to that of converting "a submarine to an aircraft, while keeping it functioning with the same crew throughout the process." While Boris Yeltsin knew how to demolish the failed Marxist ideology, he had no plan for building a new system of governance. On the political front, Yeltsin acted out two different roles simultaneously: a rebel opposed to the old Communist Party, and an authoritarian ruler presiding over a top-down regime structured like those of the Soviet past.

The US and Europe look back on Yeltsin as a democratic reformer who opened Russia to Western businesses. Russians remember his tenure during the 1990s as a time of complete chaos. A proud people, Russians watched as their nation's reputation faded in a few years from that of a powerful empire to a second-rate nation that had lost its core identity. Communism had failed; the West had triumphed.

One of the businessmen on the Christian Bridge delegation put it this way: "I came away with a heavy heart for the good people of that great country, misled by a handful of radicals for over seventy years and now left bankrupt in every area of life. I thought of it in a business sense of having a fast-talking financial advisor taking all your assets and promising great returns, but coming back one day saying, 'Well, I guess my schemes didn't work. You have lost everything.'"

The West responded with a spirit of triumphalism; it had, after all, won the Cold War. An attorney friend spent much time in Russia trying to set up a legal structure for private charities, a new concept there. As he reflects, "There was a lot of bunk about how charity could solve the few social problems that were left after the capitalist 'free market' solved the economic problems stemming from communism. In the real world, there was no way that charity could address the country's vast social needs. Within a fairly short period many Russians turned against capitalism and charity and began pining for the 'good old days' under communism."

To the average Russian, the proposed cure for communism seemed worse than the disease. Arnold J. Toynbee once likened the US to "a large friendly dog in a small room. Every time it wags its tail it knocks over a chair." American economists insisted that only a hard crash could bring about the transition from state to private ownership. Following their advice, Yeltsin made huge cuts to government spending and ended price controls.

The economy shrank, prices skyrocketed, and older Russians found that their pensions were virtually worthless.

Promises that the free market would eventually solve the nation's problems offered little solace to ordinary citizens as they carried around bags full of devalued currency in search of scarce food. A loaf of bread might double in price from one day to the next. At one point, due in large part to alcoholism and suicide, the life expectancy for Russian males sank below fifty-eight, some twenty years shorter than the norm in other developed countries.

Meanwhile, Russian oligarchs and foreign investors gobbled up Russian real estate, corporations, and energy assets for pennies on the dollar. Even as beggars and the homeless appeared on Moscow streets, a class of super rich surfaced, each with a net worth exceeding $100 million. Russia reversed its communist heritage by becoming the world's most unequal society.

The tightly controlled Soviet culture also underwent change, with an influx of Western music, movies, television, and fashion. Pornography, once forbidden, suddenly filled the newsstands and airwaves. In major cities, luxury automobiles cruised the streets, and shopping malls were now stocked with foreign-made goods. Starbucks, H&M, and KFC became household names—for those who could afford them.

Russia scholar Suzanne Massie made this observation in 1993: "During twenty years of regular visits to the old Soviet Union, I read daily vilifications of the United States. The propaganda failed; I never heard a hostile word about America from ordinary Russian folk. . . . What the Communists failed to do in seventy-four years, we accomplished in three. Today Russians identity us with the 'money disease' that has swept their country, bringing greed and crime in its wake. They call it *bucksi*."

A series of scandals plagued Yeltsin's administration as appointees began to abuse their power by siphoning money from the state treasury. These abuses sent a message that no one would be indicted for corruption, which naturally encouraged the spread of further corruption.

All these trends provoked opposition from the parliament, where Communist Party members still held a large number of seats. In 1993 Yeltsin tried to dissolve the parliament, which in turn voted to impeach him. Yeltsin sent police to surround the building and cut off its electricity. Then he called in the army. Tanks shelled the Russian White House, blasting holes in the building and killing several hundred people. For many

Russians, it was the last straw. Yeltsin had lost his moral legitimacy by using force against his opponents, just as previous Soviet leaders had done.

ॐ

Boris Yeltsin would win one more election, propped up by the financial support of Russian oligarchs. He then dropped out of view, undergoing heart surgery in September 1996 and a quintuple bypass procedure two months later. His reelection ensured that the Communist Party would not return to power, as many had feared. But Yeltsin, who had ascended to power as a reformer, now reigned as a kind of elected monarch while his family and cronies ran the country. Russians described his corruption-infested regime as a mafia state. Looking back, one American diplomat reflects, "We were focused on trying to build democracy in Russia, while the Russians were actually battling each other over power and money."

Foreign missionaries were hardly prepared for the upheavals of the 1990s. The powerful Russian Orthodox Church and its sympathizers viewed foreigners as part of the cultural invasion from the West. At the urging of the Orthodox Patriarch, the Russian parliament passed a law making it illegal for foreign religious organizations to "engage in religious-missionary publishing or advertising-propaganda activity." Though Yeltsin refused to sign the bill, the effort gave an ominous hint of things to come.

A growing nationalist movement, supported by the Russian Orthodox Church, worked to reduce the impact of foreign missionaries in Russia and successfully suspended the agreement with CoMission. Meanwhile, the Russian parliament overwhelmingly approved a new law that restricted the activity of any religious organization except for the four official religions in Russia: Orthodoxy, Judaism, Islam, and Buddhism. Excluded, Protestants and Catholics feared that a new Soviet-era period of persecution was coming. President Yeltsin vetoed the bill at first, but then signed it in September 1997.

Yeltsin's poor health, compounded by his heavy drinking, led to further distrust in government. Yet another economic crisis in September 1998 rattled the nation. The Russian people no longer trusted anyone in authority, and many blamed the efforts to build democracy in their country as the cause of their problems. Democracy had become a dirty word. Russians looked for a political savior, a strongman who could bring order to the chaos.

CHAPTER 14

Putin's Ascent

A WEAKENED BORIS YELTSIN faced a challenge: to find a successor who could win the parliament's approval without jeopardizing the wealth he and his friends had tucked away. Yeltsin's ruling team eventually decided on Vladimir Putin, a former KGB officer and low-ranking official from St. Petersburg. Putin had few supporters, no known ideology, and little charisma. But he had a record of good management and loyalty to his bosses, and he showed leadership potential. Parliament approved him as prime minister in August 1999 and subsequently tapped him to run for the presidency in 2000.

In a book of interviews published the year of his election (*First Person: An Astonishingly Frank Self-Portrait by Russia's President*), Putin recalls his early life as a tough hoodlum who fought rats in his apartment building and brawled with strangers on the streets of Leningrad. He learned that, in his words, "A dog senses when somebody is afraid of it, and bites." As an adult he bore grudges, especially against anyone who slighted his country or himself. While serving as a KGB officer in East Germany when the Berlin Wall fell in 1989, he had frantically burned documents detailing Soviet abuses. He felt humiliated by the triumph of the West.

In their book, *Mr. Putin: Operative in the Kremlin*, Fiona Hill and Clifford Gaddy discuss the difficulty of truly understanding Putin, who was a master at creating pseudo-information and suppressing other details about his life. For fifteen years after he emerged in the spotlight, there was not "a single substantive biography published in Russian, by a Russian, of President Putin." By contrast, a number of serious biographies were written about him in English. Western scholars soon learned, however, that information about Putin was controlled and manipulated. Hill and Gaddy concluded that very little is "definitive, confirmable, or reliable," and the tough hoodlum stories were probably part of the Kremlin's mythology.

Putin had never been elected to political office, and he barely campaigned before the election. Although no one knew what he stood for, the new president quickly became popular for his energy and decisiveness. He projected strength and vigor by posing shirtless as he rode horses and swam in frigid water. He cracked down on terrorists, and managed to balance Russia's budget for the first time in memory.

Putin also quickly restored law and order in Moscow and across the country. In 1995, I [John] had been accosted by two Moscow police officers, who directed me down a deserted side-street and asked to see my wallet in order to "verify my identity." They then took all my cash. It frightened me to realize that officers of the law were crooks themselves. When Putin became president, such crimes against foreigners came to an end.

Weary of the chaos under Yeltsin, the Russian people responded enthusiastically to their new leader, a man of action. Coincidentally, a spike in oil and natural gas prices brought in huge amounts of cash to Russia, a major producer. For the first time in years, Russia had a robust economy. Although the Kremlin quashed dissent and took control of the three main television networks, restrictions on free speech and laws against protest seemed a small price to pay for stability.

At first, foreigners living in Russia, including Christian leaders, welcomed the new president. During his first year in office, Putin traveled to eighteen countries and said he wanted to build constructive relations with the West. Corporate leaders and heads of Christian organizations alike agreed that Russia at last might normalize and now had the leadership to move forward on the path of reform. The country was heading in the right direction.

President George W. Bush, seeking to establish a personal relationship with the Russian president, met with Putin in a Slovenian palace in June 2001. Bush surprised Putin by asking him about a cross around his neck. Putin replied that his mother had given him the cross, which he later had blessed in Jerusalem. He had hung the cross in his *dacha*, and when fire destroyed the house, the firefighters found the cross in the wreckage. Afterward, when asked if Putin was a man Americans could trust, President Bush answered yes.

Three months later, Putin became the first foreign leader to call the White House after the terrorist attacks of September 11, 2001. Putin ended the conversation by saying, "I want you to know that in this struggle, we will stand together." Besides expressing his condolences, Putin promised that the Russian army would not mobilize to match the mobilization of US forces—the first time since World War II that one of the competing forces of the Cold War "stood down." The next day, the two leaders spoke again. Putin informed Bush that he had ordered a moment of silence across Russia and the lowering of flags to half-staff. Delegations from both countries began exploring the possibility of a new bilateral relationship.

It did not take long for the relationship to cool. Putin had expected some benefit from his supportive actions after the attacks of September 11. The only concession he received was a week's advance warning that the US would be pulling out of the Anti-Ballistic Missile Treaty. He felt Russia was not being treated as an equal partner.

The two-year friendship with President Bush began to fray when the United States invaded Iraq in March 2003. From Putin's perspective this attack, launched without the support of the United Nations, exposed the US as a superpower willing to forcibly intervene in the internal affairs of other countries. He grew suspicious that the US was also using its soft power to interfere in Russia's own affairs, especially through its large network of NGOs (Non-Governmental Organizations). The Kremlin ended such programs as the Peace Corps in Russia, and revoked the license of Radio Free Europe.

Observers referred to the Russian president as "Vladimir the Lucky," for during his time in office the government's revenues from oil companies grew from $6 billion a year to $80 billion. The surplus funded massive urban renewal projects in Moscow and other cities. The next round of elections, in 2004, underscored the president's ascendancy in Russia's politics: though he ignored campaigning, held no rallies, and offered no new plans for his second term, he still received more than 71 percent of the vote. By the summer of 2006, Russia had paid off the last of its substantial debts to Western banks and was fully solvent. Putin now felt empowered to confront the global influence of the United States.

The rupture of the Russian-American partnership became clear when Putin spoke at the annual Munich Security Conference in 2007. Putin attacked Western powers, particularly the United States, with a long list of grievances that included the expansion of NATO and the development of missile defenses in space—all of which, in his opinion, showed a superpower trying to dominate the world on its own terms. Analysts viewed this speech as a defining moment. In the seventh year of his presidency Putin had the national assets, both financial and military, as well as the confidence he needed to stand up to the West.

Back at home, where he was limited to two terms as president, Putin engineered a cunning move. He set up his colleague, Dmitry Medvedev, as a candidate for the presidency. Once elected, Medvedev appointed Putin his prime minister, thereby ensuring Putin's continued reign.

Nonetheless, by the time Putin declared his candidacy for the presidency for a third term in 2012, the country had tired of his strong-arm tactics. Tens of thousands of protesters marched through Moscow's streets calling for "Russia without Putin." He had delegated control of the economy to his cronies, so that a hundred billionaires possessed about 35 percent of the country's wealth.

Putin resented those who opposed his reelection, especially the young people who had profited financially under his policies. In response, the Kremlin began to crack down on dissent by increasing fines for public protests, shutting down opposition websites, and passing a law requiring organizations that receive international funding to register as "foreign agents." The opposition movement that had recently filled the Russian streets with protests soon dissolved.

Meanwhile, Putin had put the FSB—the Federal Security Service, a successor to the KGB—under his direct supervision, and once again its agents opened a bag of dirty tricks. Journalists reported on more than 120 targeted assassinations carried out under Putin's supervision: by letter bombs, gunshots, poison, or by his opponents mysteriously falling out of windows. The assassinations occurred not only in Russia, but in cities such as Berlin, London, New York, and Vienna. In one notorious case, Alexei Navalny survived a deadly nerve agent being planted in his underwear; medical treatment in Germany saved his life, and he courageously returned to Russia, only to face a long prison sentence.

Along the way, coziness with the West, and particularly with the United States, had ended. No US efforts to "reset" relations with Russia had any chance of success. When Putin and President Barack Obama met on the California coast in June 2012, neither displayed any signs of friendliness.

Later, President Donald Trump made overtures toward friendship, but was unable to translate them into meaningful gains for Moscow.

Putin also nursed a grudge against Western leaders' refusal to attend the Sochi Olympics in 2014 as a protest against Russia's meddling in Ukraine. After pouring $51 billion into the Olympics—the most expensive Olympics ever and the largest construction project on the planet—he felt snubbed.

Steven Lee Myers, a *New York Times* reporter who wrote a biography of Putin titled *The New Tsar*, contrasts Putin's first fourteen years in power with the years following the Sochi Olympics. In his first three presidential terms, Putin focused on restoring Russia as a major player on the global stage, while exploiting the financial institutions of the free market for the benefit of himself and his oligarch supporters. By 2014 he was rejecting the "universal values" of the West and asserting Russia's culture and traditions. Those traditions had little place for such values as democracy, individual human rights, and the rule of law.

ॐ

The pattern of oppression continues. In 2022 alone, some two dozen notable Russians died in mysterious ways, succumbing to what *The Atlantic* calls Sudden Russian Death Syndrome. The Russian victims include a sausage tycoon, a gas industry executive, the editor in chief of a Russian tabloid, a shipyard director, the head of a ski resort, an aviation official, and a rail magnate.

The clearest indication of Putin's current attitude toward the United States came on September 22, 2022, a day when he signed treaties annexing four Ukrainian regions into the Russian Federation. He made no attempt to disguise his fury.

> The West is ready to cross every line to preserve the neo-colonial system which allows it to live off the world, to plunder it thanks to the domination of the dollar and technology, to collect an actual tribute from humanity, to extract its primary source of unearned prosperity, the rent paid to the hegemon. . . . It is critically important for them to force all countries to surrender their sovereignty to the United States.
>
> I want to underscore again that their insatiability and determination to preserve their unfettered dominance are the real causes of the hybrid war that the collective West is waging against

Russia. They do not want us to be free; they want us to be a colony. They do not want equal cooperation; they want to loot. They do not want to see us as a free society, but a mass of soulless slaves.

We are proud that in the twentieth century our country led the anti-colonial movement, which opened up opportunities for many peoples around the world to make progress, reduce poverty and inequality, and defeat hunger and disease.

Western countries have been saying for centuries that they bring freedom and democracy to other nations. Nothing could be further from the truth. Instead of bringing democracy they suppressed and exploited, and instead of giving freedom they enslaved and oppressed. The unipolar world [created and run by the US] is inherently anti-democratic and unfree; it is false and hypocritical through and through.

They [the West, especially Americans] do not give a damn about the natural rights of billions of people, the majority of humanity, to freedom and justice, the right to determine their own future. They have already moved on to the radical denial of moral, religious, and family values.

Today, we [Russians] need a consolidated society, and this consolidation can only be based on sovereignty, freedom, creation, and justice. Our values are humanity, mercy, and compassion.

Vladimir Putin's hostility toward the West, and particularly toward the United States, makes clear that there is no likelihood of a thawing of US relations with the Russia while Putin remains in power. Now that we know more about Putin's past in St. Petersburg, and about his KGB allies who worked hard to promote him to leadership positions in both St. Petersburg and Moscow, it seems evident that he never had any intent to build democracy in Russia. These partners wanted access to wealth and power, and they used Putin to achieve their goals by creating an autocracy to counter the West, most notably the United States. The Russian bear, like the dog in Putin's mythical childhood, was still looking for something to bite.

CHAPTER 15

Church and State

FOR MOST OF THE twentieth century, church and state were stern adversaries in Russia. Only four Protestant churches survived the decades of atheism, and the Communist government also confiscated many Catholic properties and closed more than fifty thousand Russian Orthodox churches and chapels. Zealots destroyed some church buildings and "de-converted" others into barns for cattle and horses.

Vladimir Putin publicly revoked the hostility against the Orthodox by overseeing the restoration of thousands of their churches. Under his rule, Moscow helped reconstruct the tsarist Cathedral of Christ the Savior, a nineteenth-century masterpiece that had been dynamited under Communist rule and replaced with world's largest open air swimming pool. Furthermore, by returning confiscated property to the Orthodox Church, Putin made it the largest—and most loyal—landowner in Russia.

As a result, although Putin's popularity within Russia rose and fell, he could consistently rely on support from the Russian Orthodox Church. At the height of anti-Putin dissent, the head of the church, Patriarch Kirill, praised his leadership, declaring the Putin era a "miracle of God"—the most direct political endorsement from the Russian Orthodox Church in a hundred years.

Before Putin came to power, the Orthodox Church had found itself competing with the flood of missionaries from the West who represented many different Christian denominations. When the Christian Bridge delegation visited Moscow in 1991, we heard from Soviet leaders, including President Gorbachev, who were searching for a new belief system since Marxism had so obviously failed. Members of the Supreme Soviet and other government elites openly discussed the need for Christian colleges and universities in Russia, and no one suggested linking them to the Orthodox Church.

Some dissidents within the Orthodox Church itself welcomed the new spirit of openness. After the fall of Communism, Father Alexander Men, who had served as a priest for thirty years despite constant harassment by the KGB, began offering public lectures on Christianity to large crowds. In sharp contrast to efforts by the Orthodox Church to secure its privileged position, Father Men argued emphatically for religious pluralism and a secular state that "serves the interest of its citizens regardless of their religious affiliation." His voice was silenced in September 1990 when Father Men was murdered on his way to church by an ax-wielding assailant.

Inspired by Father Men, other reform-minded priests sought more religious freedom in Russia, but during the 1990s the Orthodox leadership resisted any possibility of true religious pluralism. When Putin later became president, he seized the opportunity to tighten control of the religious sphere in Russian life and used Orthodox theology as a weapon against any internal opposition.

It may seem an odd coupling, the Orthodox Church and a former KGB agent. One humorous exchange took place during Putin's visit to Washington, DC. The Russian president entered the Oval Office as morning sunlight was streaming though the south windows. Scanning the room as he stepped through the door, Putin blurted out, "My God . . . this is beautiful!" President George W. Bush, laughing, pointed out that was quite a response for a former KGB agent from an atheist country.

Yet Putin claims to have been secretly baptized as a child, by Patriarch Kirill's father, while Kirill himself has been suspected of working for the KGB during the Soviet era. In any event, both men profit by the close association now. Kirill gets government backing for church programs and policies while Putin gets political support from Orthodox parishioners.

With the collapse of Marxism-Leninism, Russian Orthodoxy has emerged as a substitute state ideology, one that undergirds Putin's nationalistic vision. To him, Russian Orthodoxy provides a sacred purpose for his regime's existence and backing for his dream to rebuild the Russian empire. Putin and Orthodox religious leaders jointly launched a "culture war" to protect Russia's social values, in contrast to what they regard as the decadent values of the West. Once viewed as a liberal, Putin changed his policies to align with the Church's positions on such issues as abortion and LGBTQ rights. He touts Russia as the world's leading Christian nation.

For his part, Patriarch Kirill draws a moral line against the West. "Today there is such a test for the loyalty of this government, a kind of pass to that 'happy' world, the world of excess consumption, the world of visible 'freedom.' Do you know what this test is? The test is very simple and at the same time terrible—this is a gay parade. The demands on many to hold a gay parade are a test of loyalty to that very powerful world . . ."

Russia's favoritism toward the Orthodox has meant expulsion for many Protestant and Catholic organizations. The status of religious freedom shifted dramatically in 2016 with the passage of a law "On Combating Terrorism." Ostensibly an anti-terrorism bill, this law limits foreign and domestic missionary activity and undermines freedom of assembly and speech for Russia's non-Orthodox believers.

The Kremlin views the West as a swamp of decadence and unbelief, a failed culture. Patriarch Kirill names the main threat to Russia as a "loss of faith" such as has occurred in Europe. And Vladimir Putin has accepted the role of restoring Christendom. What better place to start the purge than in Ukraine, where Russia first embraced Christianity, a thousand years ago.

Putin envisions a Russian world (*Russkiy mir*) that includes Russia, Ukraine, and Belarus, as well as ethnic Russians throughout the globe. *Russkiy mir* has a common political center (Moscow), a common spiritual center (Kiev, Ukraine), a common language (Russian), a common church (the Russian Orthodox Church, Moscow Patriarchate), and a common patriarch (Kirill), who works in harmony with the common president (Putin). This perspective casts the West as not only a political foe, but a spiritual enemy. Importantly, this perspective has no room for an independent Ukraine.

The dream of a Russian world has achieved the status of a quasi-religious cult. In one Moscow press conference, Putin said that nuclear weapons and Orthodox Christianity were the two pillars of Russian society; one guaranteed the country's external security, while the other guaranteed its moral health. In 2020 he inaugurated a cathedral of the Russian Armed Forces dedicated to war. Its khaki-colored floor is made from melted-down German tanks. On the walls, mosaics commemorate Russia's wars, including the invasion of Georgia in 2008, the annexation of Ukraine's Crimean Peninsula in 2014, and the nation's role in Syria's civil war. From the ceiling, angels smile down on the armed forces as they fulfill their holy mission.

Putin's desire to revive the grand dream of a Russian world became clear in 2023, at a patriotic rally held in a stadium packed with 95,000 flag-waving citizens, mostly young. Standing in the center of the stadium, Putin praised Russia's army by quoting Jesus: "Greater love hath no man than this, that a man lay down his life for his friends." He held up the example of a deeply religious admiral from the eighteenth century, who had helped win Crimea back from the Ottomans. The admiral, Fyodor Ushakov, canonized by the Orthodox Church, later became the patron saint of nuclear-armed long-distance bombers. "He once said that the storms of war would glorify Russia," Putin announced. "That is how it was in his time; that is how it is today and will always be!"

ॐ

I [John] lived in Moscow during the transition time between the chaotic era of Gorbachev and Yeltsin and the ascendancy of President Putin. As mentioned, I had been officially invited by Russia's Minister of Science and Education to establish a Christian liberal arts college. During these years, I experienced from the ground up the changes taking place within Russia.

As my team worked through the tedious tasks of recruiting faculty, seeking accreditation, devising textbooks, and finding classroom space to rent, my host nation seemed to implode. Boris Yeltsin ordered an armed attack on the legislature and started a war in Chechnya. The ruble's value fell like a meteor, and the country's Gross Domestic Product shrank by 50 percent. Russia went through two economic downturns similar in impact to America's Great Depression of the 1930s. Due to soaring inflation, a student who missed a tuition payment by one day might owe 20 percent more the following day.

Living through these years gave me a close-up view of Russian culture. Double-talk was a way of life, a strategy to evade the grasp of the KGB. Christian students openly cheated and plagiarized each other's papers; "We're a communal society," they rationalized. And every contractor, inspector, and bureaucrat expected bribes. Although bribery seemed the only way to get things done, we decided we would not operate illegally or by payoffs.

Our tasks of getting the Russian-American Christian University legally registered, licensed, and then accredited meant confronting government officials who would not work with us unless we paid bribes, which we refused to do. This slowed everything down—an ongoing frustration my staff shrugged off with the phrase, "This is Russia." I had worked in Washington, DC for twenty years, wrestling with government officials, and yet our work in Russia made me appreciate the relative ease we experienced in the US.

In the mid-1990s, as Yeltsin's government became more corrupt, and national chaos accompanied his heart attacks and alcohol struggles, I learned that young men who sought admission to Moscow's police academy, backed by their families, paid the selection committee members up to $5,000 for securing their appointments. For a naïve American, this was stunning—bribing your way into a police academy where you were being trained to enforce the law! This was Russia.

At times, the goal of getting a university accredited in Russia seemed unachievable. Most officials in the Ministry of Education knew nothing about private education, and there were few laws to govern these new institutions. It took us seven years to secure the school's accreditation as the first faith-based liberal arts university in Russia's history. Somehow, despite all these ordeals, in September 1996, six years after my initial trip to Moscow, the Russian-American Christian University (RACU) opened. Educational freedom in Russia had entered a new era.

Sadly, RACU's saga—and Russia's—did not end there. As we now know, a red door that swings open can also close tight. As Vladimir Putin rose to power, he began reversing many democratic trends. By his second term in office (2004–2008), Putin's increasingly hostile attitude toward the West, and especially toward the United States, began to make our work at RACU more difficult. Ministry of Education officials, who had helped us previously, became uncooperative and threatening. Radical nationalist groups targeted RACU, describing our school as a Western Protestant missionary center committed to "undermining traditional Russian values." For three years we battled lawsuits and false charges that contested our title to the land and forced delays in the construction of our new campus.

In June 2005, a crowd of 250 people demonstrated at our construction site, waving flags of the Rodina (Homeland) political party. The protesters had an intimidating guard of young men with shaved heads, dressed in black T-shirts that read "Orthodoxy or Death." This opposition continued unabated throughout 2006 and 2007, yet all their efforts to use the courts to prevent our school from locating there ultimately failed.

By 2010, the hostility toward Western institutions, particularly those with Protestant ties to the West, intensified. When RACU's educational license expired, numerous obstacles against renewal were raised and the school was forced to suspend operations for a year. That summer a perfect storm occurred: new tax regulations revoked tax exemption for the new campus facility; the Ministry of Education no longer recognized any PhDs granted by American universities for the 120 faculty, some of whom had taught at RACU over fourteen years; and a major government scholarship program offering free education at state universities decreased our enrollment substantially.

Facing the prospects of a school without accreditation, and an annual property tax that soared from $2,000 to $500,000, RACU's trustees decided to suspend the school's undergraduate program, and the new campus was sold in 2014. It was no longer possible to operate a faith-based, binational (Russian-American) school in Putin's autocracy with its close ties to the dominant Russian Orthodox Church. There was no open space between church and state.

❧

As work in Russia proved more difficult and I was labeled a "foreign agent," I encouraged the board of our foundation to shift more resources to Ukraine, which was viewed as the "Bible Belt" in the former Soviet Union. On numerous visits I met the top leadership of Protestant, Catholic, and Orthodox educational institutions, always with a warm reception.

I made these observations in my journal:

> This is one reason I fell in love with this amazing country and its vibrant young people. . . . Ukraine has one of the most robust Christian populations of any country in Europe. With one-third the population, Ukraine has more Orthodox churches than Russia. On one of my first trips, I had the privilege of meeting the patriarch of the Ukrainian Orthodox Church, which broke with the Moscow patriarch. Unlike Russia, Ukraine also has growing populations of Catholics, Baptists, Pentecostals, and Adventists. All of them were proud of how they cooperated with each other, such a contrast to what I had experienced for years in Russia.

Even in the days when a freedom of conscience law had passed under Gorbachev and Yeltsin, different religious communities in Russia failed to cooperate. The psychology of fear, a legacy of communist days, carried over into the period of freedom. The transition from living in a repressive Soviet society required a massive change of mindset. Trust needed to be restored, as well as a belief in truth.

I found a remarkably different environment in Ukraine. There, religious leaders enjoyed their partnerships and rejoiced in the diversity of Ukrainian society. For years their communities had worked together providing social services that the government could not handle. Due to its proximity to Western Europe, Ukraine had become a more open society that encouraged Western attitudes toward freedom and protest. Their postcommunist history would put this spirit to a severe test.

CHAPTER 16

A Painful Past

ON A VISIT TO Ukraine in 2018, I [Philip] was struck by the similarities between the capital cities of Kyiv and Moscow. Both had the gilded onion domes of Orthodox churches, shady parks, electric trams, cobblestone streets, elegant old coffee houses, and block after block of bland Soviet-style housing projects.

Russians make up the largest ethnic minority in Ukraine, and several million Ukrainians live in Russia. On the surface the two people groups look and sound alike. Though they speak different languages, 85 percent of the words are mutually intelligible. "Most Ukrainians know Russian," my guide explained. "Your books here are usually translated into Russian, not Ukrainian, and I have no problem reading them. In Soviet days we had to learn Russian in school, and it comes in handy when we travel to other post-Soviet countries."

During my visit, though, I could sense a major difference between the two peoples. Ukrainians have a fierce streak of don't-tread-on-me independence, hardened under years of occupation. For centuries, armies from the west (German) and east (Russian) have tramped across the flat terrain of the second largest country in Europe. Free at last, Ukrainians now express political opinions openly, with no fear that someone might be listening. At the time of my visit, their army had already been actively fighting for four years over Russia's seizure of the Crimea, and Ukrainians didn't try to hide their contempt for Russia, the last of many oppressors.

The main tourist sites in Kyiv are monuments to human cruelty. I toured the Famine Museum, a memorial to the millions of Ukrainians who died of starvation in the 1930s when Soviets took over their farms and confiscated their crops. Other museums recounted the occupation by Hitler's army in World War II, when the city of Kyiv alone suffered a million casualties—more than the total number of American casualties in the entire war.

The following day I visited a grassy ravine at the edge of the city. Today Babi Yar is a park, a peaceful sylvan setting nestled in a neighborhood of shops and houses; but the very name conjures up scenes of genocide. Babi Yar was Hitler's first act of mass murder in his campaign against the Jews. Nazi soldiers and their sympathizers rounded up the city's Jews, stripped them naked, and machine-gunned them at the edge of a cliff. Around 22,000 died the first day and 12,000 the second. More than a million Jewish Ukrainians would die in the Holocaust.

Hitler's defeat led to four more decades of Soviet occupation. When the USSR began to fall apart, Ukraine saw at last an opportunity to become independent. In 1990, 300,000 Ukrainians formed a human chain in a show of unity, linking hands along a 340-mile route from Kyiv to Lviv. The next year, 92 percent of the population voted for independence from Russia, with even the large Russian minority supporting the Ukrainian cause.

In a separate agreement, the new nation surrendered the nuclear weapons based there (the world's third-largest stockpile) in exchange for security guarantees. Notably, as one of the signatories Russia agreed to respect Ukraine's territorial integrity. The decision to release these weapons has since been a cause for regret on the part of many Ukrainian leaders, in view of Russia's repeated interventions in their country.

As in Russia, the transition from Communist Party leadership to a more democratic government proved arduous in Ukraine. So far there have been six presidents, two of whom were removed after mass demonstrations protesting election fraud. In both cases, the disgraced presidents were closely tied to Putin's regime. The failure of Putin's allies to become presidents of Ukraine thwarted his plan to bring Russia's southern neighbor under his control.

Democracy got off to a rough start in Ukraine. If you think US elections are dirty, consider that in 2004, when the Ukrainian reformer Viktor Yushchenko dared to challenge the party backed by Russia, he nearly died from a suspicious case of dioxin poisoning. Ignoring the warning, Yushchenko remained in the race, his body weakened and his face permanently disfigured by the poison. On election day, exit polls showed him with a healthy lead, and yet the government managed to reverse these results through outright fraud.

In one of the little-known twists of history, deaf people sparked a peaceful revolution in Ukraine. After the election, the state-run television station reported, "Ladies and gentlemen, we announce that the challenger Viktor Yushchenko has been decisively defeated." However, government authorities had failed to take into account one feature of Ukrainian television: the translation it provides for the hearing-impaired. On the picture-in-picture inset at the bottom of the television screen, a brave woman raised by deaf parents gave a very different message in sign language.

Natalia Dmytruk had tired of translating the official state propaganda. "After every broadcast I had to render in sign language, I felt dirty," she later explained. "I wanted to wash my hands." So, one day she decided to tell the truth. On live television she signed, "I am addressing everybody who is deaf in Ukraine. Do not trust the results of the central election committee. They are all lies and I am ashamed to translate these lies. Yushchenko is our true president! Goodbye, you will probably never see me here again."

Inspired by their translator, deaf people text-messaged and emailed their friends about the fraudulent elections. Soon other journalists took courage from Dmytruk's act of defiance and likewise refused to broadcast the party line. Spontaneous protests broke out in major cities, giving birth to what became known as the Orange Revolution. Dmytruk herself became a hero to her colleagues, who called a strike and took up the chant, "No more lies, no more lies," until the government agreed to stop censoring the news.

In the capital Kyiv, 500,000 Ukrainians flooded Independence Square, many of them camping out in frigid weather and wearing orange in support of Yushchenko's campaign colors. Over the next few weeks, the crowd swelled at times to a million. After neutral observers proved that election fraud had occurred, the courts ordered a new election, and this time Yushchenko emerged as the undisputed winner.

Skip forward ten years. Once again a Kremlin-backed candidate was serving as president. He had amassed a fortune of $12 billion and lived in a mansion complete with a private zoo, a fleet of thirty-five cars, a golf course, a floating restaurant, and an underground shooting range—while most Ukrainians were mired in poverty and the country teetered on the verge of bankruptcy. At one point, this president was tape-recorded ordering the murder of one of his harshest critics.

Again Ukrainians took to the streets, demonstrating against the president, government corruption, police brutality, and the influence of wealthy oligarchs. A huge, barricaded protest camp filled Independence Square (Maidan) in central Kyiv, and the protesters made it clear that they were not leaving until these issues were addressed. In early 2014 the clashes between protesters and riot police turned violent, resulting in more than a hundred deaths. The pro-Russian president fled Ukraine and eventually wound up in Moscow. That same day the parliament voted unanimously to remove him from office. The future of the country took a dramatic turn toward democracy and freedom from Russian intervention.

This second uprising became known as the Revolution of Dignity, or the Maidan Uprising. On my visit to Ukraine, a guide named Oleg led me through memorials to the "Heavenly Hundred" killed by police snipers firing from government buildings. Another 15,000 demonstrators were injured in the protests. "This was an internet revolution," Oleg explained. "As word spread online, taxis began offering free rides to protesters from all over the city. I set up a prayer tent in the midst of half a million demonstrators and spent sixty-seven days there. We provided a place for prayer, and distributed bread and hot tea to activists and police alike."

In her book *The Ukrainian Night: An Intimate History of Revolution*, Marci Shore described the events in the Maidan as not only a political protest, but the creation of an alternative society. Individuals organized an elaborate infrastructure with film screenings, an open university, libraries, kitchens, medical clinics, and clothing distribution centers. The people involved in these protests lived as if they were truly free, not bound by the former political constraints. Volunteers collected food, medicine, and clothing to give away free of charge to the participants. Despite its size, the encampment was clean and disciplined, and its leaders forbade all alcohol. Ukrainians will not forget that outpouring of people power, nor the deaths and injuries of those who were victims of the riot police.

In his biography of Vladimir Putin, *The New Tsar*, Steven Lee Myers identifies Ukraine's Orange Revolution as a tipping point. Popular revolts threaten autocratic rulers like Vladimir Putin, and Ukraine's rebellion combined personal humiliation with a geopolitical rebuff. Putin "nursed the experience like a grudge," Myers writes. The Russian president could not fathom that Ukrainians had rejected his handpicked candidate.

Ukraine now openly tilted toward the West and aspired to join the European Union. Putin assumed that the CIA must have manipulated the process. Similarly, when mass protests for more freedom broke out in other post-communist countries—Serbia in 2000 and the Rose Revolution in Georgia in 2003—Putin believed the United States was trying to force regime change.

Soon the "Arab Spring" swept across the Middle East, toppling more dictators from power. These revolutionary events, combined with the earlier "color revolutions," were warning signs that Putin could not ignore. With Ukraine's Revolution of Dignity in 2014, once again Russia's largest neighbor became his obsession. Massive protests began to fill the streets of Moscow itself, provoking Putin to increase repression against any opponents.

Putin's world was beginning to crumble, even as his grandiose dream of extending Russian power over former Soviet territories foundered. Then came the snub by Western leaders who refused to attend the Sochi Olympics, which was planned as a demonstration of Russia's renewed global presence. Immediately after the Olympics, in a surprise move that caught most Western leaders off guard, Putin ordered military action against Ukraine. Some experts believe his invasion of Crimea was, at least in part, an act of retaliation.

Hundreds of soldiers in unmarked uniforms—dubbed "the little green men"—captured an airport, most military bases, and government buildings in southeastern Ukraine. They took control of the Crimean parliament and installed a pro-Russian leader as their new prime minister. Initially, Russia denied involvement, but finally admitted that its special forces had led the assault. Thus began a war that has dragged on for most of a decade with the cost of 14,000 lives.

We now know that after a brief conversation with a small number of his closest national security council advisors on February 22, 2014, Putin had decided to bring Crimea back under Russian control. Several weeks later, Putin ordered a referendum on Crimea's reunification with Russia with a predictable result: 97 percent approval. The Russian parliament then passed legislation legalizing the annexation of Crimea as an "act of historical justice." In the months that followed, paramilitary units trained by Russia, and eventually joined by Russian troops, moved into the Donbas region, which had a strong pro-Russian population.

The Ukrainian government was not equipped to deter these aggressive military moves. At this point in Putin's presidency, he had decided to reassert Russia's power with or without the recognition of the West. In Russia, though, the annexation of Crimea raised his approval ratings above 85 percent.

Russian propaganda had been presenting a very different narrative, building a case for war. The media portrayed ethnic Russians in the region as a persecuted minority, oppressed by neo-Nazis. According to Russian media, Ukraine was planning the extermination of Russian loyalists in the region. Ukraine's tilt toward Europe also meant that Russia might soon be bordered by aggressive NATO forces. Most Russians now viewed the outside world as an enemy, and a siege mentality pervaded the country.

Much to the chagrin of Orthodox believers in other countries, Russian Orthodox Patriarch Kirill gave his blessing to a major conflict with Ukraine, proclaiming that "We have entered into a struggle that has not a physical, but a metaphysical significance." A priest in Rostov, a city close to the Ukrainian border, put it more bluntly, describing the Russian army as "cleaning the world of a diabolic infection."

The lack of decisive response from democratic powers in the West indicated to Putin that NATO and the United States were weakening. But within Ukraine, memories of the Orange Revolution and the Revolution of Dignity emboldened the population to stand strong against Russia. Their leaders in Kyiv committed themselves to build a well-trained and battle-ready army, as well as a reformed government.

Ukraine may have lost territory to Russia and its pro-Putin sympathizers in Donbas, but Russia could not stop Ukraine from deepening its political and economic ties with the West. The war begun in 2014 fostered a growing sense of unity among Ukrainians. No matter the cost, they wanted the freedom to shape their own future and to halt Russian intervention.

CHAPTER 17

Invasion

THE FIRST SET OF disturbing images came in September 2021 from satellites detecting unusual activity. Trains and convoys of trucks from as far away as Siberia were transporting Russian tanks, artillery, and missile launchers to the borders of Ukraine. Over the next few months, more than 100,000 soldiers moved into temporary housing in staging areas. Analysts noted the presence of hospital tents and a mobile crematorium, clear signs of preparation for combat.

When American intelligence sources raised alarms, Vladimir Putin's government dismissed them as hysterical nonsense. "All this is happening in the heads of our Western colleagues," said Russia's deputy ambassador to the UN, Dmitri Polanski. What about those satellite photos revealing mass movements of troops and equipment? He suggested they would soon return to their bases in Russia after a series of practice maneuvers.

Again and again, almost daily, Russian officials insisted no invasion was afoot. "There are no such plans," declared Russia's ambassador to the US—on February 24, 2022. "We don't threaten anyone." A few hours later, that very same day, missiles began to rain down on key cities across Ukraine. On news media, grainy satellite photos gave way to close-ups of dazed senior citizens standing outside their smoldering apartment buildings, which had collapsed in a heap, like Lego blocks. Russian ground forces attacked from three directions: in the north from Belarus, from Crimea in the south, and from Donetsk in the center of the country.

The invasion shocked many Ukrainians, who had placed their faith in high-level talks between Putin and Western leaders. Suddenly Ukrainian men between the ages of eighteen and sixty were required to register for military service. As young recruits rushed to combat areas, their wives fled with children to the western borders, where NATO neighbors welcomed them. Now the media focused on these weeping young mothers, their kids clinging to them, as they kissed their husbands goodbye and joined a convoy or train headed for somewhere, anywhere, that might offer refuge for their children.

Kyiv, the nation's capital, underwent a transformation overnight. One day it was a delightful European city with architecture influenced by Slavs, Moors, and even the French Renaissance. People walked their dogs in parks; buskers played violins and accordions; e-bikes cruised the dedicated bicycle lanes. The next day, streets were deserted as residents hunkered down in one of Kyiv's five thousand bomb shelters—a legacy of the city's tragic past.

Ignore the air raid warnings, and you risked having a Russian missile land in your apartment. Luke Harding of *The Guardian* tells of a couple rudely awakened by a screaming missile. "My legs!" cried the wife as she saw pools of blood where, a moment before, her legs had been. She died en route to the hospital.

A woman named Svetlana gave an eyewitness account similar to that of thousands of Ukrainians.

> When the war started at 5:00 AM in our town, we heard the explosions, felt the shaking, and saw half our city in smoke. All of us were afraid—and it was especially saddening to see the fear in our children's eyes. Stores were destroyed and closed. A few stayed open, but we had no money to buy food, as the shelling continued day and night. The house shook and we stayed in the cellar for weeks as our hearts almost felt as if they were leaving our bodies. I gave sedatives to the children. In the morning, we put mattresses and pillows close to them, and my husband and I went out in search of food. Once we tried to leave by train, but almost died in the crush of the crowd, as so many people were fleeing. We were finally able to leave, walking at night in freezing temperatures, when we were picked up by a bus of railroad workers who helped us get to a train station.

The invaders expected Ukraine to fall swiftly. What chance did it stand against the vaunted Russian military equipped with bombers, attack helicopters, and hypersonic missiles? Tellingly, the Russian commandos airlifted into Kyiv carried only three days' rations. On the first day of conflict, Russians seized a strategic airport near Kyiv and took control of the

Chernobyl nuclear power plant. Ominously, a forty-mile-long column of tanks and armored vehicles was advancing toward the capital.

The general who had commanded NATO during the Balkan war predicted Kyiv's fall within twenty-four to thirty-six hours. Experts in the Pentagon were more sanguine, believing the Ukrainians could hold out for a few weeks.

Day after day, images of the unfolding horrors of war dominated global news. Artillery shells falling on a nuclear power station. The bombed-out ruins of a kindergarten and primary school. A missile exploding in a crowded Kyiv shopping center. Entire civilian neighborhoods reduced to rubble. A tank obliterating a family sitting in a car. Hundreds of orphans, dazed and crying into their scarves, walking toward Poland. A train station, packed with refugees, targeted by cruise missiles. A fatally injured pregnant woman carried from a bombed maternity hospital on a stretcher.

Every day of the war, on average, five children were killed or injured. As one seventy-one-year-old civilian said, "In war, you don't get accidentally killed. You accidentally survive."

❧

In planning the war against Ukraine, Vladimir Putin and his spies in the FSB made a number of serious miscalculations, which revealed the Achilles' heel of autocrats. Because officials feared telling the leader the truth about their country's situation, honest intelligence reports were not shared with Putin. His advisors told him what they thought he wanted to hear: that the Ukrainians would quickly surrender and that Ukraine's president, Volodymyr Zelensky, would abandon the country with his family in fear for his life.

We now know that Russian forces brought with them less than a week's worth of supplies, and had no strategic plan for occupying a country with a population of 43 million. It quickly became evident that funds for updating the Russian military had wound up in the pockets of its leadership, leaving the army with a serious shortage of supplies and ammunition.

Perhaps more significant, Russia also underestimated both Ukraine's will to resist and the unexpected response from the West. In the words of Lena Surzhko Harned, a Ukrainian-American political scientist, "Putin had miscalculated. He thought he confronted a corrupt regime, like his own. Instead, he faced a nation."

President Zelensky, a comic actor, had run for office in 2019 with neither political nor military experience. He had, however, achieved renown in his country by exposing injustice and calling out corrupt politicians. The country united around him in that election, giving him 73 percent of the vote.

On the war's first day, Zelensky's advisors told him that a Russian team had parachuted into Kyiv with orders to assassinate or capture him and his family. As a precaution, lights were switched off in the government quarter. When gunfights broke out, President Zelensky and his closest officials donned bulletproof vests. *Had their president survived?* Ukrainians wondered.

That night Zelensky appeared in a video filmed on the street. "I am still here," he said. "We are all here," and he introduced his cabinet one by one. This was the first of his messages to the people of Ukraine. In contrast to Churchill's wartime speeches or Roosevelt's fireside chats, Zelensky's were recorded on a cell phone and lasted around thirty seconds. In simple, straightforward language he insisted, "This is our land, our country, our children. And we will defend it, every single inch."

"Churchill with an iPhone," one columnist called Zelensky, who would be named *Time* magazine's Person of the Year for 2022. The Ukrainian president delivered the same defiant message by Zoom to the European Union and the US Congress, and to more than thirty democratic parliaments. In the early days, when the US offered to evacuate him and his family, he replied, "The fight is here; I need ammunition, not a ride"—a quote that became a meme reproduced on coffee mugs and baseball caps. He traded his suits and ties for a dark green T-shirt and zip-up fleece jacket, casting himself as an ordinary citizen, not a tsar like Putin.

Zelensky's Instagram audience listened, and responded. Ukrainians did not lay down their weapons, as the Russians were demanding. They passed out hunting rifles and fashioned Molotov cocktails from milk bottles. It took an elite squad less than a day to retake the airport near Kyiv, thus eliminating an outpost the Russians had counted on for resupply. A group of soldiers on bicycles stopped the forty-mile armored column in its tracks, using homemade drones at night to drop explosives on the neat rows of tanks. The crews of surviving vehicles retreated into a forest for cover, cut off from their supply chain of food, fuel, and ammunition.

Raw courage proves infectious. Anne Applebaum reported in *The Atlantic:*

"Ukraine itself will never be the same again . . . thousands of people are making choices that they too could not have imagined two weeks ago. Ukrainian sociologists, baristas, rappers, and bakers are joining the territorial army. Villagers are standing in front of Russian tanks, shouting "occupiers" and "murderers" at Russian soldiers firing into the air. Construction workers on lucrative contracts in Poland are dropping their tools and taking the train back home to join the resistance. A decade's worth of experience fighting Russian propaganda is finally paying off, as Ukrainians create their own counternarrative on social media. They post videos telling Russian soldiers to go home to their mothers. They interview captured teenage Russian conscripts and put video clips online . . . every Ukrainian who lived through this moment will always remember what it felt like to resist—and that too will matter, for decades to come.

Ukraine's David-vs.-Goliath stance captured the world's attention. At the same time, the invasion also helped to unify European countries, who cooperated to supply the Ukrainians with weapons, intelligence reports, food, and badly needed medical supplies. Far from splintering the alliance, Putin's unprovoked invasion invigorated NATO. Alarmed by Russia's aggression, and shocked by the scenes of bombs falling on a European capital, the historically neutral countries of Finland and Sweden quickly applied for membership, adding to Russia's paranoia. In support of sanctions, more than a thousand Western companies exited Russia, writing off their investments. McDonald's alone closed eight hundred outlets.

Europe also opened its arms to receive a flood of war refugees. At the height of conflict, eleven million people—including half of Ukraine's children—were displaced. Some fled to safer parts of Ukraine while the rest used free train transport to travel to countries such as Poland, Hungary, Romania, Moldova, and Germany. Host families holding up "Welcome!" signs met them as they arrived with suitcases or cardboard boxes. Sympathetic European mothers left their strollers at railroad stations for Ukrainian moms to use. Polish churches organized first responders who retrieved refugees at the border, found them food and clothing, and enrolled their kids in school.

In the first one hundred days, Russia occupied more than 20 percent of Ukraine's territory—an area the size of Luxembourg, Belgium, and the Netherlands combined. Highways out of Ukraine were so clogged that some refugees had to wait in their cars for several days with no access to stores, restaurants, sanitary facilities, or places to sleep.

Yet, against all odds, within a few months the traffic flow reversed. Now, crowded trains and automobiles were heading in the opposite direction, back toward Ukraine. The Russians had abandoned their plan to "decapitate" Ukraine's government and install a puppet regime. Instead, they regrouped with the goal of securing two breakaway republics in the eastern part of Ukraine.

❧

In this strange, lopsided war, Vladimir Putin set the rules of engagement. When allies proposed a no-fly zone over Ukraine, or when the US offered Patriot missile defense systems, or Germany debated sending its Leopard tanks, Putin made dark threats, invoking his nuclear weapons. It's as if the playground bully first insists his opponent fight one-handed, then makes a further rule against blocking blows to the face.

Despite the uneven odds, through most of the summer of 2022 the war seemed a stalemate. Russian forces captured a town, only to have it retaken by Ukraine—or vice versa. Each time Russia had to withdraw from a town or city, they punished it with a devastating barrage of bombs and artillery. Short of ammunition, Ukrainian forces could fire only a hundred shells for every thousand launched against them. But they had a clear advantage in morale, fighting for their homeland against demoralized Russian conscripts who had been told they'd be greeted as liberators.

By the summer of 2022, at great cost in casualties, Ukraine began to push the invaders back. Due to its indiscriminate bombing of civilian areas, Russia had destroyed or damaged 116,000 residential buildings and 2,420 educational institutions. The organization Physicians for Human Rights documented more than seven hundred attacks on health care facilities, including 292 attacks on hospitals and sixty-five on ambulances. In the major cities, museums and historical buildings were targeted, as if to signify that Ukrainian culture was not worth preserving. So much for Russia's claim of "liberating" Ukraine.

As Ukraine proved itself on the battlefield, the US and European allies began shipping in more advanced weaponry. In August, a series of mysterious explosions took place deep inside Russian-occupied territory: a blast at an airfield destroyed ten warplanes; another airfield blew up, along with an ammunition dump at an important railway hub—the work of Ukrainian partisan forces. A crucial bridge linking Russia and Crimea collapsed in flames into the sea.

Longer-range artillery helped Ukraine advance against Kherson, a strategic city that had fallen to Russian forces on the war's very first day. "Russia is here forever," the occupiers had declared. Nevertheless, Ukraine launched counterattacks throughout the summer until, finally, Russia was forced to retreat.

As it happened, though, the Russian humiliation in Kherson was a mere sideline to Ukraine's surprise attack on Kharkiv, Ukraine's second largest city, located just twenty-five miles from the Russian border. Russia had redeployed troops to bolster defenses around Kherson, and Ukraine used the opportunity to stage a major assault on Kharkiv. In a few days Ukraine repossessed as much territory as Russia had gained in four months of fierce fighting.

The Guardian correspondent Luke Harding describes the scene in his book *Invasion*:

> The Russians fled. Their retreat was chaotic and disorderly: a pell-mell affair. Military units were abandoned, left without officers and communications. Some soldiers called their relatives and asked them to make inquiries in Moscow as to where they should go next. Others grabbed bicycles and scooters and pedaled off in the direction of home. Many departed in civilian clothes, leaving behind their tanks and armored vehicles, or were taken prisoner.
>
> The local population, almost all of it, welcomed this liberation. They hugged the Ukrainian soldiers and stood by the side of the road, cheering, waving, and kneeling in homage as triumphant Ukrainian convoys went past.

Ironically, the city of Kharkiv, home to a large ethnic Russian population, bore the brunt of Putin's revenge. After evacuating, Russian forces fired a thousand missiles against the city. A pastor there wrote, "This can't continue! It is unbearable! Our city is being wiped off the face of the earth. The explosions never stop neither day nor night. There is so much fear. It is an unbelievable, inexplicable horror that feels as if it is paralyzing every cell of an exhausted body."

What happened in Kharkiv was repeated in other towns and cities. After being forced to evacuate territory they had captured, Russian forces launched massive missile attacks against mostly civilian targets, killing

Ukrainians and Russians alike. These attacks deepened the animosity toward Russia from ethnic Russians who had previously wavered in their support for Ukraine.

Humiliated by the defeats, Putin responded with a change in strategy. Instead of pounding Ukrainian military targets, he ordered missile, bomb, and drone attacks against the infrastructure providing electricity, water, and heat. Let the people of Ukraine—including the elderly and seven million children—endure the harsh winter with no power and with inadequate supplies of food, medicine, and water. In this act of peevish revenge, he would make as miserable as possible the very people he claimed to liberate from oppression.

Putin and his national security advisors had never anticipated the response of a unified Ukrainian society mobilized in a battle for survival. The mayor of Lviv summarized the war this way: "The Ukrainian army is forty-two million people—the entire country. If ever there was a people's war, this is it."

CHAPTER 18

Dirty War

MY [PHILIP] 2018 VISIT to Ukraine took place four years before the Russian invasion. As a base for my speaking tour I stayed in Irpin, a leafy suburb of 65,000 adjacent to Kyiv. Some two dozen Christian ministries operated out of Irpin, including Youth With a Mission, Youth for Christ, InterVarsity, and Samaritan's Purse. There I got to know two men, each named Sergey, and when Russia attacked Ukraine in 2022, I began receiving regular updates from both Sergeys.

Sergey Rakhuba heads the NGO that sponsored our Christian Bridge visit some three decades before. When Russia passed the law labeling employees of international NGOs as "foreign agents," the organization changed its name from Peter Deyneka Russian Ministries to Mission Eurasia and shifted its focus to less restrictive parts of the former Soviet Union. Sergey R. had arranged the speaking tour in Ukraine and Belarus, and in 2018 I met with his Ukrainian staff in their modern headquarters building in Irpin. When war broke out, Mission Eurasia played a leading role in caring for the most vulnerable.

Sergey S., a young author I first encountered at a writers' conference, had become a long-distance friend. From the war's onset, he sent me eyewitness reports in his charming English. Sergey's faith never faltered, even when he was describing the horrors of war. Each of his emails ended with the line, "God is good. All the time." I wondered: Could I say that if I were huddled in a basement or subway station, listening to the missiles whistling overhead? As I read the heartbreaking news from Ukraine, I pictured my fellow writer Sergey and my translator Natasha, and many others I had met there. How do they sleep at night? What do they tell their children? Are they among the throngs at the border, desperately trying to flee their country?

Irpin, a peaceful bedroom community, became the unlikely site of one of the earliest battles of the war. The Russian army had planned to sweep with lightning speed through towns like Irpin in an encircling maneuver around Kyiv. They had not counted on such fierce resistance from the Ukrainian armed forces. For a solid month the two sides fought an urban battle in Irpin, with tanks clattering through the streets and gunfights breaking out in office buildings and shopping malls.

By the time Ukraine forced a Russian withdrawal, 70 percent of Irpin's buildings had been destroyed, including the headquarters of Mission Eurasia. Russian soldiers made a bonfire of its large stock of Bibles and Christian literature. Shells also damaged all five buildings of the Irpin Biblical Seminary, which was housing hundreds of refugees made homeless by the Russian assault.

A neighboring town, home of the Ukrainian Bible Society, fell completely under Russian control. In time that town, Bucha, would become known as the site of one of Russia's most notorious war crimes.

Two months after the Russian invasion, I attended a Christian publishing conference in Hungary, one of the countries bordering Ukraine. The ongoing war dominated every conversation. Ten thousand refugees were streaming into Hungary daily, adding to the half million already sheltering there. Its neighbor Poland had absorbed more than three million in that short period of time, most of them women and children or the elderly.

At the conference I heard reports from international colleagues affected by the war. A Russian publisher who lives part-time in France told me she woke up one day to find that her credit cards and ATM card had all been canceled, due to the sanctions imposed against Russia. "How am I supposed to run a business when I can't get access to money?" she asked. "Like many Russians, I hate what's happening in Ukraine. But we feel isolated and voiceless. If we speak up in our own country, we risk arrest. Meanwhile, the rest of the world has sealed us off. Planes no longer fly from Moscow to Europe, and so to get here I had to take a twenty-hour bus trip and catch a plane from Finland."

Her Ukrainian counterpart had no sympathy for the inconveniences Russians faced. She was working with human rights organizations to investigate war crimes, and daily she heard horror stories of women who had been raped and abused by Russian soldiers. "Vladimir Putin is a demon from hell," she said, her face twisted in rage. "He is destroying my country. No one but Putin wanted this war. He's the devil incarnate!"

To my delight, my Ukrainian friend and fellow author, Sergey S., also made it to the conference, driving sixteen hours from Kyiv to Budapest. He still had that winning smile, but I had never seen Sergey so subdued. A few weeks earlier, Ukrainian forces had retaken his home town of Irpin and nearby Bucha. "Philip, you no believe it," Sergey said. "The Russians, they leave mines on bodies, so if you move them—bang. Booby traps! They target ordinary peoples. Leave bombs on toys and in washing machines and even in a ten-year-old girl's piano. They plant mines in forest where I like to walk, now cannot."

Sergey asked me to video a message of encouragement on his cell phone, for a friend who had escaped from the Russian occupiers and fled to Germany. Three of her family members had been killed, including her husband. "Where's she from?" I asked. "Bucha," he replied.

Swiping his cell phone, Sergey located a drone photo of a cemetery in Bucha: row after row of graves of civilians killed, each marked with a plain white cross. "Some die from shells," he said. "Many executed—hands tie behind back, one bullet in back of skull. We find in mass graves and re-bury them, with dignity." Ninety percent of the 458 civilian bodies showed signs of shooting, torture, or violent trauma, and already the International Criminal Court was looking into the deaths.

Bucha became a turning point in public perception, as leaders from across Europe came to view the Russian army's atrocities for themselves. Investigators collected hundreds of hours of eyewitness testimony, backed up by video evidence recorded on cell phones. Snipers had shot senior citizens as they stepped outside to walk a dog, then looted their apartments. A teenage boy whose cell phone contained a photo of a destroyed Russian tank was tortured to death. Girls as young as thirteen had been raped. And the mass grave, dug hastily to cover up the crimes, held the bodies of thirty-one children.

Russia cynically accused Ukraine of staging the massacre by hiring actors to pose as corpses. Putin himself brushed aside the scenes from Bucha as fakes. But when satellite images and videos corroborated the eyewitness accounts of looting, torture, rape, and murder, the Kremlin simply stopped responding. Reviewing the evidence, an American general remarked, "This is the kind of undisciplined behavior you expect from an army in the six-teenth century, not the twenty-first."

ॐ

Ivan Rusyn, the president of the Ukrainian Evangelical Theological Society, lives in Bucha. "I used to be a pacifist," he told *Plough* magazine. "Now I believe that only the nation that has known the horror of war has the right to speak about pacifism. . . . I have huge anger toward Russians, but also pity, because one day they will find out what was going on. I don't know how they will absorb that information because it seems like they're living in a different world.

"Today we were delivering food in a smaller village, and as always happens, people started to share stories. One elderly lady shared that they were hiding in a basement and Russian soldiers entered. Her granddaugh-ter screamed in fear, and Russian soldiers pointed a gun at the child. The lady says that for the three weeks since, the child has not been speaking. Such fear and such trauma. One day Russians will be exposed to this truth; I just don't know how they will live with it."

In a separate interview, Rusyn described the scene of Bucha's libera-tion. He stood beside representatives of the Red Cross as survivors, most of them elderly, crawled hesitantly out of basements and blinked in the day-light. Their faces were blackened from open fires. For more than a month they had been hiding with no heat or electricity. They had stayed alive by eating from cans and drinking water from rusty, nonfunctional water heaters.

According to an official UN report, Russians soldiers likewise swept into Yahidne, north of Kyiv, during the first week of the war. They locked the town's entire population of 367 civilians—including seventy-four chil-dren and a ninety-three-year-old woman—in the basement of the village school. For twenty-eight days the captives stayed in that dank room with no electricity, no ventilation, and buckets serving as toilets. People had to sleep sitting up, the room was so crowded. The conditions, especially insufficient oxygen, caused some of the elderly to go insane, screaming, holding con-versations with dead relatives. When Ukrainian soldiers opened the door and let fresh air flood in, they found that ten of the older captives had died, their names and death dates recorded on the basement wall.

Vladimir Putin had declared that Ukraine has no right to exist as a sovereign state and, as the war ground on, his army acted as if Ukrainians had no right to exist at all.

At the height of the siege of Mariupol, shells exploded nonstop, every ten minutes. Only 10 percent of the buildings were left standing in that beautiful seaside town, which was formerly considered pro-Russian. Notoriously, Russian planes bombed a theater which had the Russian word for "children" spelled out in large letters on the roof. More than a thousand civilians had sought refuge there, and six hundred died. A few weeks later, a missile struck a railway station in Kramatorsk where up to four thousand civilians, mostly women and children, were waiting to evacuate the city.

Ukrainian forces found dozens of messages from children and teenagers written on the walls of a university basement. These messages gave an intimate and detailed sense of what it is like to be under such a brutal attack by Russian forces. One example:

> Hi, it's me again, Nata. We settled down in this corner, slept on chairs, cooked over a fire. Today is March 19, 2022, we're finally planning to leave tomorrow. There's no light, water, or other comforts here. We've been hiding in the basement for 24 days, basically. Shelling and missiles haunt us everywhere. PGTU [the university] took six direct hits. Mariupol is a ruin, a specter. It'll be very interesting to see how this ends, whether there will be a Ukraine. I'm tired of waking up to explosions and [missiles] screaming overhead. There's no glass [in the windows] anywhere, and it's super cold outside. I'm 17, I was planning to enroll in medical school, everyone sitting here had many plans and goals. But, unfortunately, no one needs us. No one was even planning to officially evacuate us, we're on our own, at our own peril and risk.

Apparently, Russian forces had the goal of completely destroying Mariupol, including its industrial and business centers, with the intent to rebuild it and make it into a distinctly Russian center devoid of any Ukrainian connections or cultural symbols, as they had done to other Ukrainian cities. Once occupied by Russian forces, the schools were forced to use a Russian curriculum, media outlets were forced to broadcast or publish in Russian, and Soviet-era street names were resurrected. This is what Putin was offering to the Ukrainian population. Is it any wonder why they fiercely resisted his intervention?

Kindergartens, maternity hospitals, shopping malls, evacuation buses, museums, churches—nothing was immune from the bombardment. And Bucha was merely the first of dozens of sites of war crimes. Each atrocity, major or minor, joined a dossier of eighty thousand cases of murder, kidnappings, indiscriminate bombings, and sexual assaults being investigated. This was genocide on a massive scale. In seeking to expand its colonial holdings, the Russian empire was killing many of the very people whose country would be absorbed into Putin's "Russian world."

As the war dragged on, the catalog of possible Russian war crimes grew longer and more varied.

- The UN and other human rights investigators documented hundreds of summary executions in places that Russian forces occupied. For example, after an exhaustive investigation the UN confirmed the violent deaths of 441 civilians—including seventy-two women and twenty boys and eight girls aged under eighteen—in just the first six weeks of Russian occupation. In the town of Izium, investigators exhumed bodies from 445 individual graves and one mass grave, cut into the sandy soil of a pine forest.

- The Russian military indiscriminately bombed civilian neighborhoods and attacked vehicles transporting refugees away from the fighting, in violation of international laws governing conflicts. Russia's assault on the energy infrastructure, which provides heat, water, and power to the most vulnerable, may also constitute a war crime. Russia fired more than a thousand missiles and drones at Ukraine's power infrastructure. Throughout the war, missiles and drones hit nonmilitary targets night after night—and the most vulnerable people, especially the elderly and children, were often the victims.

- Atrocities such as rape and torture have been widely reported. The BBC interviewed Ukrainian POWs who were tied and made to lie face down in a frozen field for three days and nights. All the prisoners suffered frostbite; one had all ten toes amputated, and another lost both feet. They described being tortured with wrenches tightened around their knuckles until they broke through skin and crushed bone.

- Ukraine protests the "cultural genocide" in which Russian forces, in an effort to destroy any evidence of culture, have decimated art galleries, government buildings, museums, and educational institutions. Areas of the country under Russian control have also removed Ukrainian-language books from schools and libraries.

- More than a million Ukrainians have been forcibly deported to Russia, its occupied territories, or its ally Belarus. A fourth of those are children, some of them transferred with their parents and others taken from orphanages and boarding schools.

- In June 2023, operatives presumed to be Russian demolished the huge Kakhovka dam. The resulting deluge ruined millions of tons of crops and flooded one hundred towns, forcing thousands of survivors from their homes. Key observers have pointed out that because Putin has failed in his original goal of conquering Ukraine, he has now decided to destroy the country instead. Conquest has morphed into annihilation.

In response, Russia has dismissed all accusations of war crimes. Indeed, a Russian court sentenced the opposition politician Ilya Yashin to eight and a half years in prison for "spreading false information" about the atrocities committed in Bucha. Someday an international tribunal will bring to light the massive video and eyewitness evidence documenting Russian crimes during the war.

The war brought out a stark contrast between the two adversaries. Ukraine eagerly tied in to the open internet through Elon Musk's Starlink system; Russia blocked Twitter, Facebook, and most foreign news sources. Volodymyr Zelensky hosted international observers, visited the front lines to plan military strategy, and still found time to record a nightly video message to his nation. Vladimir Putin rarely left the Kremlin and met his guests across a long, oversized table, or sometimes via video link from his bunker. Ukrainian military officers gave casualty reports and daily briefings on developments in the field; Russia kept up the pretense of a "special military operation" rather than *war*—merely using that forbidden word could earn the careless speaker a fifteen-year prison sentence.

No one knows what proportion of Russians support the war in Ukraine. Protesters filled the streets at first, but Putin cracked down hard, arresting more than twenty thousand of them. Silent protests, such as laying flowers by a statue of a famous Ukrainian poet, led to more arrests. A teenage university student faced a ten-year prison sentence just for criticizing the war on her social media posts. Many Russians voted with their feet, fleeing to places like Turkey and Finland, among them many young men desperate to avoid military service. Data from the first year of the war indicates that at least 500,000, and perhaps a million Russians fled their country. This historic exodus repeats what happened following the 1917 Bolshevik Revolution and the Soviet Union's collapse in 1991, when very few Russians ever returned. Analysts believe this emigration will redefine the country for generations.

As justification for the war, Russia gives several explanations. For domestic consumption, state media harp on the need to "denazify" Ukraine—a galling swipe at President Zelensky, a Jew who lost many relatives in the Holocaust. Pundits on Russian TV routinely refer to Ukraine as "the territory formerly known as Ukraine" and casually discuss how many millions of Ukrainians may have to die for the nation to be "denazified."

In a BBC interview, Russia's foreign minister gave a more plausible explanation. War was necessary, he said, because "we had absolutely no other way of explaining to the West that dragging Ukraine into NATO was a criminal act." Ukraine's tilt toward Europe fed Russian paranoia about facing a potentially hostile alliance within range of Moscow. The foreign minister did not, however, mention that in Soviet days the only military assaults on Russia's allies came from the east, not the west, as Soviet forces invaded Hungary and Czechoslovakia to crush their reform movements.

Few other nations accept Russia's self-justification. A week after the invasion, the UN General Assembly adopted—by a vote of 141 to 5, with thirty-five abstentions—a resolution rejecting Russia's action and demanding that Russia immediately withdraw its forces. Only four UN member states, Putin's most loyal friends, voted with Russia: Belarus, North Korea, Eritrea, and Syria.

CHAPTER 19

Holy War

To UNDERSTAND RUSSIA'S POINT of view, you must go back in history more than a millennium, to a time when the Grand Prince of Kiev, Vladimir the Great, conquered an area that encompasses much of modern-day Russia and Ukraine. A consummate pagan, Vladimir[1] had at least seven wives and eight hundred concubines, and erected statues and shrines to a variety of gods. Later, after considering various religions, he decided to convert to the Eastern branch of Christianity.

On one memorable day in AD 988, Vladimir commanded the residents of Kiev (now spelled Kyiv in Ukrainian) to come to the Dnieper River and undergo a mass baptism. Russia traces its cultural origin to that landmark event. By decree, Vladimir "Christianized" his empire and ordered that churches replace the pagan monuments.

Patriarch Kirill of Moscow underscores the importance of Kyiv to the Russian Orthodox Church. "Ukraine is not on the periphery of our church," he says. "We call Kiev 'the mother of all Russian cities.' For us Kiev is what Jerusalem is for many. Russian Orthodoxy began there, so under no circumstances can we abandon this historical and spiritual relationship."

For Kirill, the conflict in Ukraine is quite literally a holy war, one that "has not only political significance. We are talking about something different and much more important than politics. We are talking about human salvation, about where humanity will end up, on which side of God the Savior, who comes into the world as the Judge and Creator, on the right or

---

1. Ironically, Vladimir Putin and Volodymyr Zelensky are both namesakes of the prince, one using the Russian spelling and the other, Ukrainian.

on the left. . . . All of the above indicates that we have entered into a struggle that has not a physical, but a metaphysical significance."

In his newsletter *The Dispatch*, David French cites an ideological "fusion" between the Russian Orthodox Church and the FSB, Russia's intelligence service. Neither Patriarch Kirill nor Vladimir Putin sees the incongruity of dedicating an Orthodox church in the notorious Lubyanka prison building, headquarters of the FSB—the former KGB—that assassinates dissenters at will. Likewise, both leaders seem content to ignore the atrocities committed in Ukraine in view of what they see as a larger battle: withstanding the spiritual decline of the West.

French concludes, "This is the church at its worst, when it weds itself to state power and wields the sword to advance God's kingdom on earth. We are watching the deep darkness of malevolent Christendom, a religious movement that will slaughter innocents to fight 'decadence' and bomb hospitals to combat 'sin.'"

He then adds a counterpoint: "But when great evil arises, great good answers. And in this case, the great good is also in the church."

જ

The stories of war atrocities that I [Philip] heard in Hungary were made easier to bear by stories of the Ukrainian churches' response. My friend Sergey excitedly reported that his Irpin Bible Church was one of the few buildings not destroyed in that town. "We make human center, with feeding and counseling and medicine. Seven hundred peoples per day. Plus, shelter for homeless at night." In the early days of fighting in Irpin, Sergey mobilized his church to transport some two thousand refugees to safety in NATO countries.

During the first hundred days of the war in Ukraine, 183 churches were destroyed or damaged. Yet the surviving churches and schools opened their doors to provide shelter for residents made homeless by the bombings. While millions of civilians were being evacuated, many of the staff and students at seminaries and Christian colleges chose to stay behind to serve the needy.

For example, the Ukraine Evangelical Theological Seminary in Kyiv, despite being hit with six Russian missiles, reopened as a humanitarian aid center where people could get immediate assistance and hide in a basement during air raids. Kitchen personnel in the seminary refused evacuation and kept preparing food for the homeless. Mobile teams from the seminary delivered food, power generators, hygiene items, and medicines to the vulnerable.

Churches across the denominational spectrum continued to work together. Before the war, a consortium of Orthodox, Catholic, and Protestant church leaders had cooperated in a campaign called Ukraine Without Orphans (UWO), with the goal of finding stable homes for the country's thirty thousand adoptable orphans. UWO grew to involve four hundred churches of all confessions, and by 2021 the number of children eligible for adoption had fallen to less than five thousand. After the invasion, UWO worked to move the remaining orphans from war zones and relocate them in neighboring countries.

The Ukrainian Catholic University in Lviv, although damaged by Russian artillery, continued to serve as a channel for aid from the US and NATO allies. Many of its male students joined the army, while their wives and children took refuge in NATO countries. Some staff and female students, however, refused to flee and began serving free hot meals and providing places for frightened refugees to sleep.

When the Russian army occupied Kherson and other towns and villages in southern Ukraine, that region suffered a humanitarian crisis, a shortage of medical supplies. Ignoring the risk, Christian volunteers began transporting medicines and equipment through dangerous Russian checkpoints. Mission Eurasia staff distributed two thousand wood-burning stoves to help those who had lost power for heating and cooking. They also sponsored twenty mobile kitchens that can feed three hundred people per day

Aleksei, a doctor at a home for the elderly recalls,

> When Russian troops entered the city, all the medicines in pharmacies disappeared. We knew that we'd be able to help our elderly patients for a maximum of ten days using what we had stored up. But after that, without life-saving medicines, our elderly were doomed. I never thought that Christians in our country would have such unity and would serve people so passionately. Our "God-believers," as we called them, contacted their fellow believers in western Ukraine, and in a few days we had all the necessary medicines. It was then that I started believing in God who saves people through His followers.

Joni and Friends, the organization founded by Joni Eareckson Tada, relied on its European partners to evacuate some four hundred Ukrainians with disabilities. Those who needed special care went on a four-day bus trip to the Netherlands, which offered accessible housing. Bus drivers lifted paraplegics in their arms and carried them up the bus steps to their seats. Some drivers even changed the soiled disposable underwear of children with disabilities. A Dutch board member reported, "We are giving them shelter, medical attention, clothing, and food—including cakes decorated with the Ukrainian flag that say, 'You are safe with us.' They come traumatized, but after a day of food and rest, their mood changes 100 percent."

❧

In Kyiv, seminary faculty, staff, and students practiced "the ministry of presence" while serving the free hot meals. They sat beside the strangers who showed up, listened to their stories, and provided comfort and pastoral care. Now the seminary is training lay counselors in a six-week program designed to help church members learn how best to listen to the war stories they hear and how to counsel the traumatized, especially the elderly.

The need for a ministry of presence came home to me [Philip] when I received a letter from the publisher of some of my books in Ukraine. Alex lives in Zaporizhzhia, a city of 710,000 that had absorbed 200,000 refugees, many of them from regions where the battles were severe. He wrote, "Although they might not have a scratch on their bodies, they are all deeply wounded emotionally. The amount of sheer terror and anguish they've experienced exceeds the limits of human endurance. So, not only do they refuse to demand anything, they often do not talk at all. They stare ahead with glassy eyes, or periodically start sobbing without tears, apparently having lost any interest in every aspect of life and human connection.

"Each of the families who meet with the Christian counselors every day has a heartbreaking, even unimaginable story," he wrote, and recounted a few:

> Here's a young woman from the small town between Zaporizhzhia and Mariupol whose husband served as a captain in the army. When the Russians came to town, she was raped repeatedly for several days by the soldiers—before the eyes of her thirteen-year-old son. The boy has stopped speaking since then. Somehow, they both, the mom and her son, managed to flee from the occupation. "I'm going to divorce my husband," cried the woman. "I just

couldn't stand this shame." A few days after she'd settled in the new place, she received a "killed in battle" notice about her husband.

Another family arrived from the same area, a couple in their thirties expecting a baby in a few months. After six weeks of occupation, they were finally able to flee. All that time, the husband had been hiding in their house, to avoid being forcefully drafted into the Russian army. Meanwhile, his pregnant wife worked as a nurse at the local hospital. Each day she had to walk to the hospital and back via Russian roadblocks, ignoring the indecent glances and jokes from the soldiers. One day a recruit from Chechnya made a pass at her. He offered to marry her, and announced he would visit her soon. Sure enough, he showed up at her house the next day. As he knocked on the door, the couple managed to escape through the rear window, cross the backyard, get in the car, and drive out of town under heavy shelling all the way up to Zaporizhzhia. They arrived safe but they'd lost the baby on their way. Later they showed to volunteers a tiny body wrapped in cloth in the trunk of their car. They haven't spoken with each other ever since and the wife, who blamed her husband, wants a divorce.

How can you help all these people? How to ease their pain, and bring them back from the dead-end their anguish led them into? How to break through the heavy curtain of grief which blocks their souls? Moreover, how to tell them about God's love and compassion, of His presence right in the middle of their situation?

"As it happens, there's a remedy," Alex continued. "The first and foremost task for volunteers is to get these damaged people to talk; otherwise, you have no access to them. At the beginning, nothing seems to work. The refugees just start crying. One of the main problems of the suffering person is that pain shrinks the whole world into a point. How do you expand their horizon back, to awaken any interest in the outer world?"

The volunteer counselors learned a new method. Instead of asking about the victims' stories, they started telling true stories about other people who have suffered, including some from books.

> For some readers, their enormous pain begins to gradually dissolve in the other stories of suffering they've heard or read. They start talking. They soften and even relax a bit. They start telling their own stories in more detail. They let the pain out and burst into tears. And then they start asking questions themselves . . . and even become ready to listen to answers. Not everything happens during the first conversation, but amazingly they seem willing to come back again and again.

It is hard, of course, to see the seeds sprout soon. Some of the refugees resettle in distant places, and we lose touch. Yet, most are fairly easy to follow: they want to stay near, and periodically visit the refugee centers for humanitarian aid—but also to grab further books, and to speak with a Christian counselor. Some show up in church in a week or two . . . including those two families I mentioned above. The lady with a thirteen-year-old son has even started preparing for baptism.

We experience suffering alone—it "islands" us. Somehow a shared tale of suffering, and recovery, reconnects a lonely person to the rest of humanity. A glimmer of hope appears.

One year into the war with Russia, the theologian Miroslav Volf at Yale Divinity School conducted a podcast interview with his former student, Fyodor Raychynets, a pastor who also teaches at Ukraine Evangelical Theological Seminary. He described the weariness of sleeping on the floor of his office (safer than his home), enduring winter days with no heat or electricity, and living with the constant terror of bombs and missiles. "We cannot see light at the end of the tunnel," he said. "My church is in Bucha. We have a saying, 'When we die, we are sure we will be in heaven because we have already been through hell.'"

Raychynets, too, speaks of a ministry of presence. When he visits soldiers on the front lines, they thank him for the humanitarian packages he brings, but say they really want a chaplain, someone to stay with them and pray with them in their suffering and despair. The UN chose Raychynets's church as a major distribution point for its food program. A church that had averaged 150 in attendance before the war suddenly found as many as a thousand people crowding into the building on Sundays. "We knew why, of course: they came because of material need, not spiritual."

But to his surprise, when the program ended, the people kept coming. "Even now we have five hundred to six hundred on a Sunday. My sermons have changed. I can't say 'as the Bible says' without explaining, because they don't know the Bible. I have to be blunt, and clear, as if talking to a foreigner. I have to tell them I don't have an answer to their questions when I don't. We offer a safe space for emotional outpouring, and encourage our people to find someone else who has suffered and share it. Some have lost family and are looking for new family, or have lost friends and are looking for new friends."

Pastor Raychynets ended his conversation by referring to Jesus' parable of the wheat and the tares. "Yes, we have to fight evil, but the most effective way to fight it is to be good, a wheat and not a tare. . . . We just have to be a people of dignity and with dignity we should face the trial that has happened in our lifetime. We just have to be the kind of people that will not turn [into] something else rather than human, but rather will become a better human."

It will take years, perhaps generations, for Ukrainians to have a sense of recovery, for themselves or for their devastated nation. Meanwhile they endure, clinging to shreds of faith in their future, and pride that, against all odds, they have not been defeated. Above all, they hope that the world does not forget them or the painful lessons they have learned. British historian Timothy Garton Ash credits Ukraine for teaching us all that sustaining freedom requires constant vigilance, because "freedom's battle is never finally won."

PART FOUR

Lessons Learned

by John A. Bernbaum

CHAPTER 20

Culture Counts

WE HAVE SEEN HOW, in a series of popular uprisings, Ukraine fought fiercely for democracy following the collapse of the Soviet Union. Some of the fourteen other former Soviet republics also became more democratic, but others clearly did not. This pattern baffled Western observers. After the brutal regime of Stalin and his successors had been exposed, why didn't Russia and other Soviet republics repudiate dictatorial leadership and one-party rule? Instead, they reverted to a form of top-down control with little freedom of speech and no strong commitment to human rights.

Journalists and political analysts in the West focused almost entirely on political and economic reform efforts. In view of the opportunities for new political parties and NGOs, they assumed that these emerging countries would move toward democracy and free-market economies as the natural best step. In the process, they ignored the underlying culture, especially the moral and ethical breakdown that had occurred in communist states. They were blind to the signs of spiritual renewal and deaf to the cries of the people.

It doesn't surprise me [John] that Western observers overlooked the moral and spiritual crisis that undermined communism. After all, religion holds little interest for secular scholars. It does surprise me, however, that they disregarded moral and spiritual factors even when Communist Party leaders involved in the drama emphasized them.

In his bestseller *Perestroika*, Mikhail Gorbachev discussed the reasons for his and his colleagues' "new thinking" about restructuring the Soviet Union. In the late 1970s, Party leaders realized that the country had begun to lose momentum, as if a kind of "braking mechanism" was slowing progress. In addition to economic stagnation, Gorbachev warned against the "gradual erosion of the ideological and moral values of our people." He noted that a "breach had formed between word and deed," causing a decay in public morals.

The author of *Perestroika* laid down a clear agenda: to rebuild Soviet society, including its moral life. In Gorbachev's own words: "Today our main job is to lift the individual spiritually, respecting his inner world and giving him moral strength. . . . *Perestroika* means the elimination from society of the distortions of socialist ethics, and the consistent implementation of the principles of social justice. It means the unity of words and deeds, rights and duties." In effect, Gorbachev was proposing a moral and spiritual revolution.

During his visit to the Vatican in 1989, Gorbachev again made his views explicit. He said:

> We need spiritual values, we need a revolution of the mind. This is the only way toward a new culture and new politics that can meet the challenge of our time. We have changed our attitude toward some matters—such as religion—that, admittedly, we used to treat in a simplistic manner. . . . Now we not only proceed from the assumption that no one should interfere in matters of the individual's conscience; we also say that the moral values that religion generated and embodied for centuries can help in the work of renewal in our country too.

Gorbachev understood well the moral and ethical crisis of Marxism-Leninism. So did his colleagues. Of many examples, I will cite only one. Fyodor Burlatsky, one of the leading reformers in the Soviet Union, a man who was chosen by Gorbachev in 1987 to head the new Soviet Public Commission for International Cooperation on Humanitarian Problems and Human Rights, put it this way:

> The Soviet Union has to be a free country where everyone can pray to his or her own god. In fact, religion has to play a role in our return to elementary moral values. There have been so many crimes and so much corruption in our history, nobody knows what the foundation of morality is anymore.

Professor Harold Berman of Emory University was one of the few Western scholars who had both eyes open and got it right. He summarized the crisis: "The collapse of communism was primarily a moral and spiritual collapse." Berman noted that Russian Christianity was "a significant factor in what the Gorbachev leadership in 1987 and 1988 began to call 'democratization.'" He continued: "Atheism lost because it deprived the Russians of the spiritual beauty and power and the elements of transcendence and of personal salvation which they crave."

❧

Why did other Western scholars fail to grasp what Professor Berman saw so clearly? Throughout Eastern Europe and the former Soviet Union, they largely missed the moral and cultural revolution that contributed to the fall of communism. Religious leaders paved the way for the dramatic, nonviolent changes that occurred throughout the Soviet empire. Inspired by the courage of Pope John Paul II, countless Christians actively worked in human rights groups and humanitarian organizations, building a groundswell of support for democratic change.

The Cold War, observed former US Senator Sam Nunn, ended "not in a nuclear inferno, but in a blaze of candles in the churches of Eastern Europe." Indeed, the fall of the Berlin Wall traces back to candlelight processions in East Germany. Activists would begin with a prayer meeting at a church, and then march in the street, holding candles and singing hymns. In Leipzig, first a few hundred, then a thousand, then thirty thousand, fifty thousand, and finally five hundred thousand—nearly the entire population of the city—turned out for the vigils. In East Berlin a similar march attracted one million protesters, and that was the night the Berlin Wall came tumbling down without a shot being fired. A huge banner appeared across a Leipzig street: *Wir danken Dir, Kirche* (We thank you, church).

Most Western analysts passed over this important dimension of the revolutions from 1989 to 1991. For example, the prestigious journal *Foreign Affairs* published twenty-one articles concerning these events, and only three of them mentioned the role of the church. Likewise, other leading journals, such as *Foreign Policy, World Politics,* and *The National Interest*, failed to credit the cultural factors underlying the political revolutions. A moral and spiritual awakening had been underway for years. Despite one of the most systematic persecutions that Christianity has ever experienced, religious faith did not die out in the Soviet Union, but rather began showing signs of vibrancy and renewal during the 1970s and 1980s.

During my many trips to Russia from 1990 to 1993, I repeatedly asked local university students to name their favorite books. One book stood out with no rival in sight: Mikhail Bulgakov's *The Master and Margarita*.

133

This brilliant novel, written in 1940 but not published until 1967 because of opposition from Soviet censors, weaves together three stories. The first concerns a love story about an author (called "the Master") and his girl-friend Margarita; the second gives a delightful satire on life in Moscow in the 1930s, in which a professor of black magic (who is Satan portrayed as Professor Woland) causes havoc with his supernatural powers; the third story depicts the encounter between Jesus and Pilate leading up to and including the crucifixion.

I met several Russian students who had read this book twenty to twenty-five times. If I had to summarize a book as complex and intricate as *The Master and Margarita*, I would say one of its central messages is this: *only a fool believes there is no God.* Writing under the oppressive censorship of the Stalinist period, Bulgakov ironically used Satan's testimony to prove the existence of God. The popularity of this book among university students in the early 1990s gave me cause for hope in Russia's future.

Many other examples from the creative arts and mass media reveal the crisis that Marxist-Leninist ideology was undergoing. Chingiz Aitmatov, the popular writer from Kirghizia, wrote a pointed essay in *Pravda* in February 1987. Seventy years of Soviet power, he said, had succeeded in removing Christian values, but had failed to replace them with anything positive. He charged that Soviet society was devoid of "compassion" and dominated by a ruthlessness that destroyed social justice concerns.

Films also gave evidence of the dramatic changes occurring in Russian society. Philip Yancey has already mentioned *Repentance*, a surrealist allegory of the cult of Stalin. Written in the early 1980s and produced in 1984, the film was not released until 1986, eighteen months after Gorbachev came to power. Its appearance caused a political earthquake.

In our own history, the United States had three primary cultural influences shaping society: the classical legacy of ancient Greece and Rome, the European Enlightenment, and Christianity. The Founding Fathers, well-schooled in these historical movements, knew that democratic capitalism depends on values such as trust, integrity, and accountability. Government is not the highest authority in the country, but operates under the rule of just laws. Most importantly, the American Declaration of Independence proclaims that certain unalienable rights are "endowed by their Creator." American society is grounded in respect for the rights of individuals because humanity was created in the image of God.

The assumption that democracies will spontaneously arise out of the chaos following the overthrow of foreign dictatorships has repeatedly proved misguided. We saw this during the "Arab Spring" when few of the affected Arab countries became democracies. The same pattern held true in most of the post-communist states that were a part of or allied with the Soviet Union. If the underlying culture does not share a respect for integrity, trust, and openness, the seeds of democracy will not germinate. Culture matters, and must be addressed if there is any hope for the creation of a democratic society.

ॐ

The Russian prophet Aleksandr Solzhenitsyn may be the most insightful guide to the collapse of communism in 1991 and to Russia's flawed attempts at democracy. As early as 1965, Solzhenitsyn predicted that "Time has finally run out for communism." He repeated his prediction when, nine years later, he was forcibly exiled from his homeland. Not only did he accurately describe what would happen to the Soviet regime, he also played a vital role in bringing about its demise.

In November 1962, *Novy Mir*, one of the leading Soviet literary magazines of that time, published Solzhenitsyn's *One Day in the Life of Ivan Denisovich*. The novel made him world-famous overnight and, as Professor Edward Ericson noted, "broke the official conspiracy of silence about the greatest horror story . . . in human history." Solzhenitsyn would go on to chronicle that horror story of Russia's oppression of its own citizens, which in his calculation had cost sixty million lives.

In the early 1970s, Solzhenitsyn and a circle of like-minded Russian intellectuals published a book of essays describing the difficulties that beset the country and suggesting long-range solutions. The central thesis of their essays, published in English under the title *From Under the Rubble*, asserted that the problems of the modern world—Western as well as Soviet—could no longer be solved on the political plane. Rather, solutions must be sought in morality and religious faith. They proposed a "moral revolution" in Russia, one that rejected physical violence and compulsion.

In an article titled "Repentance and Self-Limitation in the Life of Nations," Solzhenitsyn argued that repentance had historically been a characteristic of Russian life, nurtured by Russia's rich Christian tradition. This capacity for repentance had withered because of the "suppression of the

Russian spirit" that began in the days of Peter the Great. By the twentieth century, "the blessed dews of repentance could no longer soften the parched Russian soil, baked hard by doctrines of hate." The violence and hatred generated under the Soviet regime for seventy years led to the loss of the "gift of repentance" in Russian society. Eventually, the very notion of repentance attracted ridicule.

Rather than point the finger at others for Russia's tumultuous past, Solzhenitsyn offered a profound insight into evil: "the universal dividing line between good and evil runs not between countries, not between nations, not between parties, not between classes, not between good and bad men: the dividing line cuts across nations and parties, shifting constantly. . . . It divides the heart of every man." In light of this truth, Solzhenitsyn argued that Russians need to stop blaming others for their troubles and start reflecting on their own errors and sins, asking for forgiveness for the evils they have committed. In his judgment, repentance is "the first bit of firm ground underfoot" and "the only starting point for spiritual growth."

Insisting that Russia's struggles were not the result of external forces, Solzhenitsyn acknowledged that Russians "have done evil on a massive scale and mainly in our own country, not abroad, not to others, but at home to our own people, to ourselves." Further, if Russians want to move forward "to build a just, clean, honest society," the only way to shed the burden of the past is to repent and confess that "we are all guilty." Solzhenitsyn believed that even the cleverest economic and social reforms could not convert "the kingdom of universal falsehood into a kingdom of universal truth." Only repentance can do that.

Rather than focusing on the loss of the Soviet empire, Solzhenitsyn called for internal reform, "the healing of our souls." In his judgment, "we must stop running into the street to join every brawl and instead retire virtuously into our own home so long as we are in such a state of disorder and confusion." One strategic place to begin the reform process is in school, the "key to the future of Russia."

Solzhenitsyn had a mission to speak the truth to those in power. Professor Ericson observes that although Solzhenitsyn described the horrors of Russia's past, he always ended his books on a note of hope. If contemporary horrors stem from the fact that "men have forgotten God," then change is possible once people put their faith in God. This insight stands as a profound warning, not only for Russia but for all civilizations.

Those of us who took part in the Christian Bridge trip in 1991 heard leading members of the parliament and *Pravda* journalists describe Russia's principal challenge as spiritual, not economic or political. We also heard our KGB host, General Nikolai Stolyarov, make this stunning statement: "There can be no *perestroika* apart from repentance. The time has come to repent of that past. We have broken the Ten Commandments, and for this we pay today." Like Solzhenitsyn, Stolyarov had clear eyesight and good hearing. Later, General Stolyarov would oversee the distribution of 1.5 million New Testaments to the Russian armed forces.

The interviews with Soviet leaders and members of the intellectual elite during our visit to Moscow were truly unique. These Russian leaders now saw that religion was not a negative force, but a healing solution. The deep spirituality of their culture, repressed and distorted by Marxism-Leninism, needed to be revived. We shared this hope, but as Gorbachev and reform-minded members of parliament were gradually removed from power, the light of hope began to dim.

After our delegation left Moscow, it did not take long to see that Boris Yeltsin had no real plan for democratizing the Russian government. Soon he began acting like earlier Soviet leaders. His family and key partners gained access to government resources, and corruption became a recurring problem. As the economy faltered, politicians adopted the theme that Russia was a victim of the West. Meanwhile, the Russian people clung to the memory of the glory days of the Soviet empire and dreamed of restoring it, a dream that persisted through the chaotic 1990s. When Vladimir Putin came to power in 2000, the Russian economy rapidly recovered, giving new momentum to the drive to expand Russian power and prestige.

Putin and his St. Petersburg KGB colleagues worked to rebuild a centralized Russian state, which controlled large segments of the economy. They had no interest in rebuilding the moral and spiritual basis of Russian society. Without a cultural reformation, Russia reverted to a top-down governing system that had little participation by the Russian people.

The seeds of democracy have little chance to survive when the cultural soil is rock hard and soaked with the blood of its own people. And when the fear of chaos reigns, any promise of law and order sounds appealing.

CHAPTER 21

"Who Are We?"

WHEN THE USSR COLLAPSED in December 1991, fifteen post-Soviet states faced the enormous challenge of remaking their countries. Now independent, they also had the unique opportunity to choose a new self-identity. Russia and Ukraine chose markedly different paths, and the consequences of their choices are still playing out conspicuously on the global stage.

In Russia a deep mood of dissatisfaction led many to question the most fundamental traditions and beliefs of Russian society. Desperate problems, suppressed for decades by totalitarian deception, had suddenly come out into the open. Meanwhile, the pace of rapid change created a sense of social turmoil. British Historian Geoffrey Hosking once described Russia under Stalin as The Land of Maximum Distrust. He characterized the new mood as *anomie*, or a "vacuum of values" (borrowing a term from Emile Durkheim). This vacuum resulted in a sharp increase in crime, violence, and suicide, as well as a proliferation of bizarre beliefs and aberrant behavior. Astrology, for example, spread virally in the new Russia, and most predictions by astrologers were darkly pessimistic.

For centuries Russia had existed as an empire ruling over others; the concept of a cohesive nation with its own identity had not fully developed. The euphoria of 1989 to 1993, an early period of fascination with Western democracy, ended in disillusionment, and Russians had little agreement on what lay ahead. In 1996, President Yeltsin proposed an unusual contest. He sketched the various stages in Russian history—monarchy, totalitarianism, and Gorbachev's *perestroika*—each with its own ideology. The current democratic path of his government lacked a clear identity, he said, and so he initiated a public search for "Russia's soul," offering a prize of ten million rubles ($2,000) for the best essay on a "unifying national idea." In effect,

Yeltsin was conceding the mood of *anomie* in his country after the failure of communism and the limited success of *perestroika*.

The ensuing struggle for identity proved frustrating, for Russians couldn't even settle on the basic symbols of a nation. After two years of debate, their national anthem still had no lyrics because the Russian parliament refused to approve them. The parliament also rejected the tri-color (white, blue, and red) flag and the two-headed eagle, which some deputies opposed because of its connection to Russia's pre-revolutionary past. When Moscow celebrated its 850th anniversary in September 1997, the police had to rehang many of the tri-color flags, because some municipal workers had inadvertently hung them upside down.

Debates over public symbols and monuments typified the confusion in Russia over its national identity. A proposal to remove Lenin's body from Red Square stirred passionate debates, especially among the elderly. Most Russians did agree, however, that a loyalist's plan to send Lenin's corpse on a world tour in order to turn a quick profit was a bad idea.

As Russia entered the new millennium, the basic question about identity remained unsettled. Many in the West assumed that when the Soviet Union collapsed, a new nation would automatically form out of the ruins. But too many basic questions lingered: *Who are we as Russians? What are the natural borders of the Russian state? How can we live together when the Russian Federation includes so many different ethnic groups? What kind of state best fits this reality?*

In previous centuries, during the reign of the tsars, Russians had an ongoing debate about national identity. "Westernizers" believed Russia should follow the European path of development. "Slavophiles" argued that Russia was distinct from Europe and should carve out its own path. Still others saw Russia as a Eurasian power, straddling both Europe and Asia.

The two-headed eagle that now symbolizes the Russian Federation illustrates Russia's uniqueness: one eagle faces west and the other east. Yet the two-headed eagle also represents the problem: Russians cannot figure out where their identity is grounded. Are they true Europeans who need to catch up with their neighbors to the West, or should they forge their own separate destiny?

When the Communist Party came to power in 1917, its leaders proclaimed a model of a socialist society populated by "New Soviet Men and Women." Rulers of the USSR boasted that their experiment in social engineering, not an import from the West, represented the wave of the future.

The argument between Westernizers and Slavophiles quieted—until the horrors of the gulag were exposed.

When Vladimir Putin came into office in March 2000, he too had to acknowledge the failure of communism. He articulated a new path for Russia's future, one based on patriotism, restoring national unity, and a strong central government, but with no "official state ideology in Russia in any guise." As the Russian economy rapidly improved, Putin's popularity rose with it. His energetic leadership made a strong contrast to the ailing Yeltsin, overweight and afflicted with heart disease and alcoholism. Putin restored pride in the country's economic success and its emerging presence in international circles. Gaining confidence, he openly criticized the West, singling out the United States for what he viewed as the unchecked hubris of a superpower.

When Putin returned to power in 2012, coinciding with a dip in Russia's economy, he became more assertive in confronting Western democracies and suppressing any domestic opposition to his regime. Putin orchestrated a series of "wars of choice" in Georgia, Chechnya, Syria, and Crimea, aggressions that alarmed democratic leaders in the West. His efforts to restore the Russian empire also rattled neighboring countries, even as he grew more paranoid about NATO members on Russia's borders.

As hostility toward the West became a dominant theme in the Kremlin, Putin obsessed over Ukraine, Russia's southern neighbor. The Revolution of Dignity in 2013–2014 was a personal defeat for Putin and he began to focus on undermining Ukraine's legitimacy. He ordered the drafting of new history textbooks that ignored the separate existence of both Ukraine and Belarus in their earlier history. Instead, they were presented as branches of "one Russian people."

By the time Russia invaded Ukraine in February 2022, no firm answer had been given to the question: *Who am I as a Russian?* Increasingly, to be a Russian under Putin meant being anti-Ukraine. A colonial war against Ukraine was now Russia's primary goal—not building a consolidated nation with freedoms of speech, assembly and worship, or even preserving the country's cultural legacy of world-class literature, music, and ballet. All that was set aside in the urge to reconquer former parts of a shattered empire.

৯৩

Until recently, many history courses in the US treated Ukraine as a part of Russia, rather than as a territory of Russia's colonial empire. Actually, Ukraine's history and culture are radically different from Russia's. The name *Ukraine* means *borderland*, and because of its geographical location Ukraine has suffered from centuries of foreign invasions.

Beginning in the sixth century, Greeks, Romans, and Byzantines established colonies on the northeastern shore of the Black Sea, while eastern Slavs moved into the central part of what is today's Ukraine. In the thirteenth century, Mongolian forces defeated the regional Slavic powers. After Mongols vacated this area, for the next six hundred years Ukraine's land was ruled by competing empires, including the Polish-Lithuanian Commonwealth, the Austrian Empire, the Ottoman Empire, and the Romanov dynasty in Russia. When Putin talks about Ukraine's permanent ties to Russia, he is inventing a false narrative to justify his aggression.

Global media have highlighted the harsh reality that wherever Russian forces occupied Ukrainian territory in 2022 to 2023, they left behind evidence of torture chambers and mass graves. The invaders made no attempt to hide the atrocities, for they were intended to intimidate the Ukrainian people. These well-documented atrocities will likely result in numerous trials for war crimes.

Less well-known is the cultural genocide that Russians have pursued since the beginning of the war. Hundreds of libraries and archives have been damaged or demolished, and thousands were forcibly closed. In addition, Russian soldiers have destroyed countless Ukrainian history books and literary works written by native writers, and have removed hundreds of valuable textbooks from school libraries. Irreplaceable volumes and manuscripts have been taken from museums and churches and burned.

The tragic character of this assault of cultural genocide was brought home to many Ukrainians when the body of Volodymyr Vakulenko was unearthed in a mass grave in a liberated city in the Kharkiv region. He had been kidnapped, beaten, executed by two shots from a Russian pistol, and buried with 446 other victims. Vakulenko, who had an autistic son, wrote popular children's books; the bestseller *Daddy's Book* tells of a hardworking elephant named Slavka who tends a garden full of crocuses and dahlias. Inspired by Vakulenko's death, many citizens have been working hard to protect what's left of their cultural heritage.

Andrey Kurkov, a Ukrainian author of novels (translated into thirty-seven languages), television scripts, and children's books, has observed that

Ukraine was fortunate for its geology but, sadly, not for its geography. Its wealth in minerals and huge expanses of fertile land has attracted a succession of empires that have claimed Ukrainian land, coal, and oil. But no empire in this region has wanted to steal one dimension of Ukraine's wealth: its rich culture. Instead, they have worked hard to eradicate it. Joseph Stalin, for example, liquidated over seven hundred of Ukraine's finest writers, politicians, and cultural activists.

Ukraine has faced attempts at cultural genocide for more than four centuries. Invaders have tried repeatedly to make Ukrainians forget their native language and their country's history, and even to stop singing Ukrainian songs.

For more than three centuries, the Romanov dynasty of Russia suppressed Ukraine's distinct culture. When Ukraine was a part of the Russian Empire, Romanov tsars signed more than forty decrees restricting or prohibiting the use of the Ukrainian language in the region that is now Ukraine. Here are just a few examples:

- In 1720, Peter the Great banned the publication of any book in the Ukrainian language.

- In 1763, Catherine the Great demanded that Ukrainian not be used at the country's oldest university, Kyiv-Mohyla Academy.

- In 1804, all teaching in the Ukrainian language was forbidden.

- In 1884, Tsar Alexander III banned any theater performances in Ukrainian.

- In 1888, the tsar made it illegal to give a Ukrainian name to a child at baptism.

After the revolution of 1917, Ukraine experienced a short period of independence, but when it became one of the fifteen republics of the Soviet Union, the process of Russification revived yet again. Under President Putin, the policies of the Romanov tsars are being resurrected and enforced in the occupied territories. Books in the Ukrainian language have been purged from libraries and schools. And in Russia, where camps have been built to house Ukrainians forcibly removed from their homes, these displaced people are being taught Russian traditions and customs to turn them into "Russian people."

Following the country's independence from Russia in December 1991, Ukrainians resolved to protect the sovereignty of their country, resisting the kind of oppression they had experienced at the hands of Communist Party leaders. When Putin intervened in Ukraine's presidential elections and tried to get one of his cronies elected as its president in 2004 and 2013–2014, the will of the Ukrainians solidified, and they decided to fight to the death to preserve their struggling democracy.

I visited Ukraine during the 1990s, and when I returned on several trips after 2016, I noticed a dynamic change among the Ukrainians I met, especially the university students. The people I encountered have a passion for their country. They fervently desire to see it become a strong democracy, with meaningful political and economic reforms and an end to endemic corruption. Unlike Russians, the Ukrainians have an answer to the question "Who Are We?" They want to live in a multilingual, multicultural, religiously diverse democracy, without any foreign interference, especially from Russia.

The war reflects a generational struggle between Ukrainian and Russian leaders. President Zelensky and many of his colleagues are in their forties, and have the strong support of the first fully post-Soviet generation, the "Independence Generation." Putin and many of his closest advisors are over seventy years old, and these Russian leaders are looking backward, trying to resurrect the former Soviet Empire and its glory days of the past. They represent two distinct generations of leaders—one committed to a future hope and the other to an idealized past.

Russia's core identity, formed through a history of living under fear-based totalitarianism, contrasts sharply with Ukraine's spirit of independence and freedom. Even so, a clash with Russia was not inevitable. Many countries manage to live in relative peace with neighboring states that have a very different government and culture. Few Russians had an appetite for war with Ukraine in 2022. Rather, the invasion can be traced directly to the consequence of granting ultimate power to an autocrat. Vladimir Putin had the ability to work out his personal grudges, and to pursue his exalted ambition for Russia, in utter disregard for the horrific cost Ukraine—and his own nation—would bear.

CHAPTER 22

The Threat of Autocracy

RUSSIA'S INVASION OF UKRAINE will be remembered as a declining empire's misguided attempt to conquer a neighboring state. Far more was at stake, however. Vladimir Putin sought to dismantle the international order created in Europe after World War II. At its core, the conflict represents a battle between autocracy and democracy.

When the Cold War ended, competition between rival ideologies faded away. Weighed down by its centrally controlled economy and top-down political style, Marxism-Leninism in the Soviet Union had lost its rivalry with democracy and a free-market economy. But in the twenty-first century, a new threat has emerged in global politics: an alliance of dictatorships that the Pulitzer prize-winning historian Anne Applebaum describes as "Autocracy, Inc." This network of dictators operates by stealing the wealth of their countries and parking these massive financial resources in banks in the West where, ironically, they are protected by the rule of law.

Autocrats around the world follow a playbook of three main strategies: populism, polarization, and deception. First, they win popular support by exploiting the weaknesses in democratic states and blaming elites for corruption and poor leadership. Once in power, they polarize the political system by sweeping away any middle ground between themselves and their opponents. Before long, they begin expounding lies and half-truths to undermine the checks and balances in government. Attacks on the free press usually follow.

The trend is spreading globally, among major players such as North Korea, China, and Iran, as well as in many smaller countries that mimic them. Autocrats get their cronies to buy media companies, which they convert into propaganda machines. They then use local media to deceive their people and to plant seeds of distrust in traditional state institutions. Such manipulation helps them gain support from people who believe their lies and become fervent fans.

In most cases, the autocrats' regimes are not run by a solitary villain. As Anne Applebaum explains, autocrats build "sophisticated networks composed of kleptocratic financial services, security services (military, police, paramilitary groups, surveillance), and professional propagandists." Corrupt, state-controlled companies in different countries work with each other and share propaganda resources. They have no common ideology, and no one person leads this group. They allow their countries to become "failed states," with ruined economies and mass poverty, while they spend huge sums of money buying property in the West, building luxurious yachts, and vacationing at the world's most expensive resorts.

Thoughtful analysts describe Putin's Russia as a "personalist autocracy," which means it centers on one person's power, and not a military cohort, political faction, or ideology (as in North Korea, China, or Iran). Recent history has shown the serious cost of losing office in such a system: 80 percent of personalist autocrats who lose power have ended up in prison or exile, or dead. As Timothy Frye notes, autocrats like Putin can enjoy their stolen wealth (which experts estimate in Putin's case to exceed two hundred billion dollars) only if they retain the power to protect it. As a result, they have "strong incentives to resort to extreme measures to prevent a transfer of power"—such as starting a war and redirecting the people's attention away from problems at home. As Frye says, "Putin's team will cling to power for the same reason that all personalist autocrats do: the fear of what comes next."

In recent years scholars have studied the weaknesses of autocracy, and their findings give valuable insight into Russia and other dictatorships. First, autocrats who undermine their country's state and private institutions (for example, courts, bureaucracies, legislatures, and media outlets) become personally vulnerable. Putin appeared to make decisions alone or with a small group of loyalists from his national security council. When autocrats believe they are the smartest person in the room, their cronies will only present information designed to please, not to tell the truth. In the case of Ukraine, it quickly became apparent that Putin had been misinformed about the Russian army's competence and the Ukrainian people's will to resist.

Reports indicate that very few people had access to Putin. Autocrats put their accomplices into positions of authority, rewarding individuals who may not be competent to run a government department or agency. Putin naturally chose loyalists whom he judged incapable of engineering a coup against him. Again, his isolation posed a risk: Putin seemed as surprised as anyone when his old friend, Yevgeny Prigozhin, led the Wagner group on a short-lived march to Moscow—"a stab in the back," in Putin's words. Not long afterward, Prigozhin died in a suspicious plane crash.

The second weakness stems from the inherent tension the autocrat must manage between satisfying the elites who support him while also keeping the general population content. As we've seen in recent years, political cabals can organize coups, and mass public protests can unseat dictators. Pleasing the two constituencies can be tricky—for example, if the elites' stolen wealth appears threatened by the dictator's risky military actions even as the bodies of young soldiers pile up in Russian cities.

The third weakness comes to light as autocrats handle repression. Coercion can be costly if overused. Putin's early popularity increased his authority as president, but that popularity will decline as the Russian economy stalls and the country becomes a pariah in the opinion of the rest of the world. Harshly repressive measures will only weaken him further.

The few Russians who spoke out did so from exile. For example, Mikhail Pavlovich Shishkin is a prominent Russian writer, the only author to have won the Russian Booker Prize, the Russian National Bestseller award, and the Big Book Prize. Shishkin lives in Switzerland with his family, and after the 2022 Russian invasion of Ukraine, he responded, "Putin is committing monstrous crimes in the name of my people, my country, and me. . . . In Putin's Russia, it's impossible to breathe. The stench from the policeman's boot is too strong."

In a letter to a Ukrainian friend, Shishkin wrote, "Do dictators and dictatorships breed slave populations or do slave populations breed dictators? Ukraine was able to escape from this hellish circle, to escape from our common, monstrous, bloody past. For this reason it is hated by Russian impostors. A free and democratic Ukraine can serve as an example for the Russian population, which is why it is so important for Putin to destroy you."

❧

Catherine Belton's book *Putin's People: How the KGB Took Back Russia and Then Took on the West*, documents the story of Putin's rise to power. She shows how high-ranking national security executives helped Putin each step of the way as he gained increasingly powerful positions in St. Petersburg and then Moscow. These executives also engineered events and terrorist actions that helped Putin stay in power, making sure to bloody his hands so he could not dare relinquish his leadership role. Putin's KGB (now FSB) cronies had a plan to take over the government and get their share of the country's wealth, a scheme they justified as a way to prevent the West from seizing control of the country's rich oil assets.

When elected president in 2000, Putin rebuilt the Russian state bureaucracy, for it had become dysfunctional by the end of Boris Yeltsin's presidency. He also dramatically enlarged the nation's national security establishment, which includes the military as well as intelligence gathering and law enforcement agencies. Russians refer to this national security network as "*siloviki*," which Western analysts translate as "guys with guns" or "men of power."

Funding for both internal security agencies and the defense ministry comprises 30 percent of Russia's national budget. Experts estimate that the number of personnel at Russian internal security agencies increased by 10 percent after the mass protests directed at Putin's reelection. Russians live in a very repressive environment, one that tolerates no opposition. The brutal treatment of protestors, even the elderly, demonstrates how these various agencies compete to outdo each other in proving their loyalty to Putin and his security council.

In addition to usurping Russia's free press—a top priority for Putin, and an example copied by other autocrats—Putin also worked to exert control over the oligarchs who had profiteered during Yeltsin's administration. With Yeltsin sidelined by heart problems and worsening alcoholism, the oligarchs had exploited their contacts with Yeltsin's family and key government officials, and were rewarded for underwriting Yeltsin's surprise reelection victory in 1996.

Putin let the oligarchs know that they could keep their wealth if they stayed out of Russia's politics. And if they didn't? He made that clear as well. He forced several oligarchs to go into exile and took over their media empires; he imprisoned another oligarch and nationalized his private oil company. The remaining oligarchs prospered, fully aware that their wealth was now tied to their devotion to Putin. When Western sanctions were introduced in 2014 (a response to Russia's involvement in Ukraine), many of these oligarchs lost their profitable contacts in the West. Putin responded shrewdly, offering them financial help in the form of huge state contracts to rebuild Russia's military-industrial complex and other major infrastructure projects.

With the help of his KGB cronies, Putin took personal control of all military and security forces. The military and its top brass, who had previously overseen foreign and defense policy, became Putin's servants. The Russian president, not the parliament, now decides all questions about the deployment of the country's forces.

I have mentioned a slide in Putin's popularity as the economy began to falter in 2008. Putin returned to the presidency in 2012 in the face of massive public protests. Playing a card used by many demagogues, Putin turned to warfare to rebuild his personal support. Aggression against Ukraine in 2014, which included the seizure of Crimea, restored his popularity ratings even as he clamped down on "enemies"—both foreign powers and domestic "traitors." Noting the Western democracies' lukewarm response to his move into Crimea, Putin concluded—wrongly, as it turned out—that NATO and the United States were weak and unlikely to oppose him.

By now, Western leaders know that Putin's attack on Ukraine's democracy was a war of choice and that Putin's rationale for the attack was based on lies and a false historical narrative. *Protecting the rights of Russian speakers in Ukraine?* That argument was ludicrous, since Russian speakers in Ukraine are much freer than in Russia. For a leader who has an interest in his country's history and who seems to view himself as another Vladimir the Great, Putin should know that wars of choice often start well but end badly. Aggressors who invade another country frequently underestimate what it takes to win, or whether battlefield success will truly benefit the leader's regime.

Russian history provides many cautionary examples of military setbacks leading to regime change—Putin's greatest fear. Defeat in the Crimean War of 1853–1856 resulted in the new tsar, Alexander II, instituting major reforms and freeing the serfs. The loss to Japan in 1903–1905 forced Nicholas II to form a constitutional monarchy, only to find himself replaced in 1917. The setbacks in World War I created the opportunity for the Bolshevik coup in 1917. Russia's disastrous war in Afghanistan opened the door for Gorbachev's reforms and the collapse of Communist Party rule. Apparently, Putin skipped over these lessons from his country's own history.

The Ukrainians did not roll over and lay down their weapons as Putin's intelligence sources had predicted. Instead, they put up a heroic resistance, which unified their country in unprecedented ways. From the war's first days, elderly women threw Molotov cocktails at Russian tanks and Ukrainians used their phones to inform their armed forces about the invaders' positions and movements. Russia's southern neighbors would not give up their country without a fight. Having endured enough Russian intervention and oppression, they were willing to risk their lives for the cause of freedom and independence.

In an unexpected consequence, the invasion has likewise helped to unify NATO countries, who cooperated to supply Ukrainians with weapons, intelligence reports, food, and badly needed medical supplies. NATO and the European Union demonstrated a unity that I am sure Putin never expected, just as he did not anticipate President Joe Biden's ability to bring these partnerships together.

Putin also badly miscalculated when his attack on Ukraine undermined his own country's energy sector, which had taken three generations to build. He thought that Europe needed Russia far more than Russia needed Europe, insisting that Europe would never survive a winter without Russian oil and gas. He was wrong. To his surprise Germany, which got two-thirds of its gas from Russia, completely cut off its Russian supply. Other European countries also worked hard to find other sources of energy. Some analysts believe that Russia will never again be an energy superpower. This demonstrates again a weakness of autocracies: if the autocrat believes he's the brightest person in the room and proves wrong, the consequences can be severe.

Arguably, Putin miscalculated what it might take to govern Ukraine, even if he were able to subjugate the land. Ukraine, roughly the size of Texas and with a population of forty-three million, would be very difficult to control militarily and politically. The Ukrainian government has organized reservists and provided weapons to civilians who have been trained to fight urban and guerrilla warfare. Any long-term occupation will result in major casualties for both Ukrainians and Russians.

Putin's attack on Ukraine's democracy will be for him a "forever war," as long as he remains in the Kremlin. He will use Russian military force, sabotage, disinformation, cyberattacks, and even bribery, if needed, to prevent Ukraine from flourishing as a democratic nation on Russia's border. Michael McFaul, the former US ambassador to Russia, has it right: "The Kremlin will remain committed to undermining Ukrainian (and Georgian, Moldovan, Armenian, etc.) democracy and sovereignty for as long as Putin remains in power and maybe longer if Russian autocracy continues."

As the Russian military invasion faltered and their forces were withdrawn from the area surrounding Ukraine's capital city of Kyiv and then other key cities, analysts raised the possibility of Putin's removal from power, especially as the death toll of Russian soldiers mounted and the country's economy suffered from Western sanctions. It is difficult to know how and if Putin might be removed from power, either by leaders of his security forces or because of massive public protests; both seem unlikely as I write this in late 2023. There have been very few coups in Russian history, and only two since the Bolshevik Revolution of 1917.

Under Putin, with the layers of security protecting him, the likelihood of a coup appears remote. Yet, autocratic rule can quickly collapse, and the Wagner group's march on Moscow revealed weaknesses both in Putin and in the nation's defenses. After twenty-five years of working in Russia, my predictions about the future have often proved wrong. When I came to Russia in the early 1990s, I was told "In Russia, nothing is as it seems." That turned out to be true.

Regardless, personalist autocrats like Putin are almost always replaced by autocratic successors, rarely by democratic leaders. Removing Putin from power, sadly, will not change the threat from Russia; it is driven by hawkish military leaders who compete to show how hostile they are to the West and how desperate they are to protect their stolen assets. Figures at the top have all supported Putin's war and have helped themselves to the wealth from Russia's natural resources and from their government's finances.

In my opinion, Europe's last empire must be defeated militarily. While there is some risk that Putin's downfall could result in the disintegration of the Russian Federation, its continued survival is a much greater threat. The US and its NATO allies can supply all the military and financial support that Ukraine needs to end Russian occupation of its territory. Rather than a "frozen conflict," which would allow Russia to reorganize and resupply its armed forces for future attacks on Ukraine and other neighboring states,

Russia needs to learn a decisive lesson on the battlefield in order to end their reign of terror.

Just as importantly, Ukraine's victory as a nation that emphasizes freedom and diversity will plant a model of successful democracy in Eastern Europe. Ukraine can celebrate with pride the freedom they have fought so hard to defend. Ukraine's global allies, especially those on Russia's borders, will join the celebration—and other autocracies just might get the message.

❧

Certain voices on both wings of the political spectrum oppose additional funding for Ukraine's war effort. For insight, I rely on the Institute for the Study of War, based in Washington, DC. In April 2023 the Institute issued a report titled "Reframing the US Policy Debate on a 'Long War' in Ukraine." The report made these principal arguments, answering some of the questions raised in our domestic political debates.

- By supporting Ukraine, the United States is not facing a "long war" in Ukraine because the US is not a direct combatant in this war. "Ukraine is defending itself against an unprovoked Russian invasion, and the US is supporting Ukraine. Comparisons to Iraq or Afghanistan are not appropriate."

- "The US is not fighting a proxy war." Ukraine asked for support from the US and the European Union because Russia launched a genocidal attack against its people, and Western allies agreed to support their struggle—one which Ukraine would have undertaken with or without support from other democracies.

- "The West and Ukraine are not protracting or spreading this war: Russia is." Putin and his national security elite invaded Ukraine in order to secure their hold on political power in Russia and to protect the assets they have stolen from the Russian people. It was entirely a "war of choice." Russia continues the conflict, which is costing the lives of many young Russian soldiers, and Putin "can choose to end it at any point."

- The Kremlin—and especially its president—has made it clear that Russia will also seek to control other countries in this region, particularly Belarus and Moldova, with the larger goal of weakening NATO and undermining the US. Other countries at risk include the Baltic states, Georgia, and other nations that Putin believes belong in the restored Russian empire. "The Kremlin is rallying Russian society for a long fight against the West."

In an essay in *First Things*, George Weigel concluded, "Now, after a year marked by bestial cruelty on one side and astonishing courage on the other, the Russian war on Ukraine stands before us as a pivotal moment in contemporary history. . . .What Ukraine means for the United States is that there is no holiday from history and no escape from world politics for America and Americans."

I recognize that pacifists and those with pacifist leanings oppose our nation's involvement in war. The needs are so great that there are many nonmilitary ways to give humanitarian support to the people of Ukraine in the massive task of rebuilding their country. Ukraine needs our help.

CHAPTER 23

Baptizing Caesar

FOR MORE THAN A thousand years the Russian Orthodox Church has played a major role in the world's largest country. During most of that time, the church enjoyed a close relationship with the state; indeed, in the days of Peter the Great the church functioned as a department of the government. The Romanov royalty were involved in selecting the patriarchs, religious leaders who rarely if ever opposed the rulers or advocated for the most vulnerable in society. Romanov tsars were, in effect, "baptized Caesars": rulers who served as the supreme authority in the empire with the blessing of the Orthodox patriarch and his bishops.

As a result, when the Communist Party gained control of the country at the end of World War I, the Russian Orthodox Church became one of the principal targets of the Bolsheviks. Historians estimate that during the first six years of Lenin's rule, the Bolsheviks killed twenty-eight bishops and 1,200 priests. There are reports of Orthodox priests being dragged out of their churches, tied to the church gates, doused with water, and left to freeze to death in the bitter cold of Russia's winters.

In the decades that followed, most of the 54,000 Russian Orthodox churches were destroyed, closed, or converted into warehouses, barns, and factories. Many of Joseph Stalin's millions of victims died specifically because of their faith. Aleksandr Solzhenitsyn estimated that, in all, sixty million Russians died at the hands of their own government between 1917 and 1987. Human history had never seen extermination on such a massive scale—and the Russians did it to themselves.

Despite the Bolsheviks' original intent to create a secular "new Soviet man and Soviet woman," Stalin—a former seminarian—realized that the spiritual longings of the Russian people could not be quenched. In response, he attempted to introduce a cult of Lenin as the Marxist Messiah. He designed Lenin's funeral and his tomb on Red Square to simulate religious symbolism; the tomb itself resembled an altar. National holidays replaced religious holidays, and various Party celebrations tapped into the religious longings of the Russian people.

In view of Russia's history with religion, it was a truly epochal event when Mikhail Gorbachev, the head of the Russian state, granted full religious freedom to all Soviet citizens and honored the Russian Orthodox Church in 1988, the thousand-year anniversary of Christianity in Russia. The USSR had been founded as a secular state, its militant atheism firmly grounded in Marxist-Leninist thought, which identified religion as "the opium of the people." For seventy years, Communist leaders had sought to deify Lenin as the god of a quasi-religion—a god that failed.

The previous year, in 1987, Gorbachev had given an address in the Kremlin's Palace of Congresses that was televised to the entire nation. In that speech, on the seventieth anniversary of the Bolshevik Revolution, Gorbachev surprised everyone by talking openly about Russia's past failures. He laid bare the truth about Stalin's purges and blamed the enormous losses in World War II on Stalin's failed leadership and his secret pact with Hitler. One Communist Party leader, after hearing Gorbachev's speech, angrily confronted him, saying, "[You] are opening the way for people to spit on our history." Gorbachev indeed opened that door.

Imagine what this must have been like for the average Russian to hear: *You have been living a lie! Your parents have been teaching you lies! Your schoolteachers have been teaching you lies!* Almost overnight, everything Russians had been taught to believe was exposed as deceit, undercutting how Russians understood their history, their role in the world, and even their own personal identity and worth. Meanwhile, Russians now had the freedom to explore religion, to attend worship services, to hear evangelists (both Western and Russian), and to read books that had previously been forbidden.

Recognizing the failure of Russia's policy of militant atheism, Gorbachev had the courage to reverse it, against the wishes of many high-ranking Party leaders. In October 1990 the Soviet government adopted "the Law on Freedom of Conscience," which "guarantees the right of citizens to decide and express their attitudes toward religion . . ." (Article 1). In addition, "no compulsion of any kind is permitted when a citizen decides his own attitude toward religion or to the confession or nonconfession of a religion, or to participation or nonparticipation in divine service and religious rites and ceremonies, and in religious instruction" (Article 3).

This transition to freedom of religion went largely unnoticed in the West. Many have written about the collapse of communism and the triumph of democracy. Many have written about the failure of planned economies and the superiority of the free market. But what about the failure of atheism? Mikhail Gorbachev recognized that the Soviet state could not eliminate religion from Russian society and that Christians were making important contributions to their country. He realized that a new political and economic order required a new moral foundation. Religion had much to offer his vision of a New Russia, and Gorbachev decided to act on his convictions.

∂❧

As a Westerner visiting Moscow for the first time in 1990, I was struck by the irony of an atheist regime headquartered in the Kremlin, amid magnificent cathedrals with their gilded, onion-shaped domes. Before Moscow was set afire by Russians as a defensive move when Napoleon approached the city in 1812, hundreds of churches dotted the nation's capital. Even today, one is struck by the number of active churches in Moscow and scattered across the countryside.

As detailed in Philip Yancey's report on our Christian Bridge visit in 1991, Russian leaders of the Supreme Soviet and even at the KGB made a remarkable confession. They admitted they had failed to understand the true character of faith, and now believed Christianity was needed to hold their disintegrating country together. In response, several of us shared with our hosts how the greatest writers of Russian literature—Leo Tolstoy, Fyodor Dostoevsky, Mikhail Bulgakov, and Aleksandr Solzhenitsyn, to name just a few—had nourished our faith and changed our lives. We encouraged them to rediscover the deep-seated spirituality in their own culture.

In the years immediately following the collapse of Communism, interest in religion soared and many new churches flourished across the former Soviet Union. But in 1992 and 1993, the mood began to change. The newfound interest in religion started to wane, churches declined in attendance, and a mood of cynicism and despair crept in. The great hope stirred by unprecedented freedom in Eastern Europe and Russia soon turned sour.

When President Yeltsin ordered his army tanks to fire on the Russian White House in 1993, suppressing a coup attempt, people realized that rebuilding Russian society would require a long struggle. They saw that Yeltsin, like many Russian leaders before him, was willing to use force against his opponents. More than anything else, this event undercut the moral authority Yeltsin had gained two years earlier, when he led the resistance to the coup against Gorbachev.

The fall of Communism created a huge moral and spiritual vacuum in Russia, a vacuum that overpriced gym shoes and Western jeans could not fill. The feverish pursuit of material possessions from all over the world, suddenly available in Russian stores for the first time, did not satisfy the hearts of Russians. Western materialism, so attractive at first, lost its initial appeal.

The churches of Russia were also unprepared to cope with societal changes. Church leaders, after living through decades of severe persecution, had a hard time adjusting to the freedom they now experienced. Experts describe this condition as the "psychology of persecution." After years of secrecy and defensive maneuvers to protect their congregations from police or KGB informants, it was difficult for these leaders to open their arms to new, unknown visitors. As a result, many Russians left traditional churches because they did not feel accepted.

Russians and Eastern Europeans began searching for new gods to replace the god of communism. The traditional Christian faiths—Orthodox, Catholic, and Protestant—attracted some interest because they were no longer forbidden, but that interest did not last. At the same time, Russian churches did not always welcome "seekers," those curious about Christianity but ignorant of the appropriate behaviors and rituals practiced in the traditional churches.

We must not overlook one more significant factor dampening the quest for faith: the long-term impact of seventy years of militant atheism. The harsh persecution of Christians under the Soviet regime did not crush the church, but it did plant seeds of doubt in the minds of many Russians about the importance and truth of any religion. The subsequent failure of Marxism-Leninism made many young people skeptical of any ideology.

Despite the diligent work by thousands of Western missionaries and Russian evangelists, a major spiritual revival did not occur in Russia. The anti-religious doctrines espoused by the Communist regime for two generations, combined with distrust of leaders and a general confusion over what to believe, made the spread of Christianity a very difficult task.

∂♥

Soon an unlikely new voice could be heard in Russia and most of Eastern Europe: a form of Christian nationalism. Fanatical nationalists formed an alliance with conservative Russian Orthodox Church leaders and former Communist Party functionaries. This "Red-Brown" (Communist-Fascist) coalition offered disaffected Russians a new faith in a resurgent Russian empire, bolstered by its Orthodox heritage and the power of the Russian army. Harking back to the days of Tsar Nicholas I, whose key slogan was "Orthodoxy, Autocracy, and Nationality," this troika of forces (Nationalists, Communists, and conservative Orthodox leaders) pushed through laws restricting religious freedom and retracting many of the freedoms granted by the 1990 law and the Russian constitution.

Communist Party leaders, who never apologized for the vicious persecution of the church during the Soviet period, began worshiping with Orthodox leaders and lighting candles on Orthodox holy days. Today, Communist Party leaders publicly declare that they see no contradiction between communism and Orthodoxy. While some concede that Lenin made "some mistakes" in his relations with the church, they still regard him as a great historical figure.

The new religion in Russia once again involves the baptizing of Caesar—this time not the tsar, but the president, Vladimir Putin, who in turn counts on the uncritical support of the patriarch of the Russian Orthodox Church and its entire hierarchy. The new creed: To be Russian is to be Orthodox. Since very few Russians attend worship services (less than 2 percent attend church on Easter, for example), Orthodoxy is a cultural identification for most Russians, not an indication of religious belief and commitment.

While Russian laws identify four official religions in Russia—Christianity, Islam, Buddhism, and Judaism—Russian Orthodoxy is the dominant, state-supported religion. Putin and his national security advisors advocate a mono-religious culture that defines the Russian world. From their perspective, the Moscow patriarch is their equivalent of the pope in Rome, and the independent Ukrainian Orthodox Church should be eliminated. Following the invasion of Ukraine, an estimated five hundred churches have been damaged or destroyed by Russian armed forces. The Ukrainian Orthodox Churches are viewed as rebel institutions that broke from Moscow's leadership, and the evangelical churches in Ukraine are accused of being full of "American spies."

Russia's history with the church offers a cautionary tale for those of us in the West. For centuries, the Russian Orthodox Church enjoyed the coziest of relations with the tsars. Its patriarchs failed to speak out on justice issues, such as Russia's wars of aggression and an economic system that lavished wealth on the upper classes while serfs lived under a form of slavery. The backlash under communism nearly, but not quite, destroyed the Russian church. When militant atheism proved to be a bankrupt ideology, the state revived a nationalist religion that once again endorses Russia's wars of aggression and says nothing about corruption and the amassing of wealth by oligarchs.

We are experiencing similar tensions in the US, with candidates making campaign speeches about reclaiming "Christian America." Right-wing political leaders are "baptizing" their candidates, referring to them as messiahs, and staking their hopes on access to power. Simultaneously, from the left wing of our political spectrum, we hear calls to remove religious discussions from the public square. Religion may be acceptable if you keep it private—but this kind of privatized religion should be no more acceptable to Christians than talk of "Christian America."

Martin Luther King Jr. used to say that the church should function neither as the master of the state nor its servant, but rather as the conscience of the state. Russia has consistently failed that test, and its recent history shows the consequences.

CHAPTER 24

What Went Right with Ukraine?

As Philip Yancey describes earlier in this book, the Christian Bridge delegation in 1991 left Moscow convinced that Russia was moving toward freedom and democracy. Mikhail Gorbachev had spearheaded some major reforms, including free elections uncontrolled by the Communist Party apparatus. Together with efforts to dismantle the centralized economy, these reforms offered for real change. In addition, the new freedom of religion had broken the close ties between Marxism-Leninism and atheism. The Russian government officials we met with saw religion as a force that could help hold their chaotic country together.

It soon became clear, however, that any radical change in the governance of Russia faced serious obstacles. A form of "imitation democracy" developed in the early 1990s, but with limited backing. Russians had a long history of autocratic rule over a vast colonial empire, with little participation by ordinary citizens in civic life. The notion of cultivating the seeds of democracy in arid soil across eleven time zones had few enthusiastic supporters.

The history of the Russian Orthodox Church added to the challenge. Many of us who visited Moscow in 1991 could sense that we were walking on blood-soaked ground. We knew about the imprisonment and execution of millions of Russians—especially the persecution of people of faith—during seven decades of Communist Party rule. No one had been held accountable for these crimes against their own people; there had been no Nuremberg-style trial or Truth and Reconciliation Commission. Except for Gorbachev, no prominent Russian leaders had expressed regrets about these atrocities. And now, in a Mephisthophelean twist, the very church that had suffered so much suddenly became a de facto part of an expansionist government.

Meanwhile, Ukraine's escape from the shackles of communism took a very different course than Russia's flawed attempt. Over the centuries, the cultural influences from Poland, Lithuania, Austria, Hungary, Germany, and Turkey—along with immigrant Jews and Greeks who settled in its southern regions along the Black Sea—allowed Ukrainians to shape their own unique identity. The country's culture grew as rich as its soil. By the nineteenth century, Ukrainians valued freedom and individualism, a contrast to the Russians' bent toward stability and compliance with autocrats. Diverse religious communities contributed to Ukraine's distinctive culture, particularly in the western part of the country that had felt the impact of the Reformation and Counter-Reformation.

The last 120 years of Ukraine's history have seen a series of atrocities, which Timothy Snyder details in his book *Bloodlands*. First, Ukrainians witnessed the collapse of the Romanov dynasty in 1917 and the subsequent Russian Civil War with its massive loss of lives. When the Communist Party seized control, Ukraine was made a Soviet republic, and underwent a deliberate famine in 1931–1933 that took five million lives. Less than ten years later Ukraine, caught between Hitler's Nazis and Stalin's Red Army, became an infernal battlefield.

After World War II ended, Ukraine once again confronted the Soviet effort to suppress any distinctive Ukrainian culture. When the Soviet Union imploded in 1991, Ukraine quickly asserted its desire to separate from the Russian empire; 92 percent of the electorate supported Ukraine's independence as a sovereign nation.

No playbook existed for converting a top-down political and economic system to a democracy with a free-market economy, and each of the fifteen former republics of the Soviet Union struggled with the transition. Ukraine's economic slowdown was devastating: the nation lost 60 percent of its gross domestic product and suffered from hyperinflation that soared as high as 10,000 percent. Much like other post-Soviet states, Ukraine saw a small number of well-placed oligarchs gain control of state property, becoming extremely powerful and wealthy in the process.

Ukraine's free-market economy underperformed due to massive corruption and mismanagement. In the 1990s, three million Ukrainians emigrated from their country to escape the mayhem. After Vladimir Putin came to power in Russia, he immediately began to intervene in Ukraine's political life. This led to the Orange Revolution of 2004, an event that signaled an important change in Ukraine—and also angered Putin, who had assumed his candidate would win, giving him an ally in Kyiv. Ukrainians showed that they wanted a future tied to Europe, one no longer dominated by Moscow.

The positive image of Ukraine's Orange Revolution elevated the country's status among its European neighbors, and the new president of Ukraine made friendly relations with the European Union a priority. Freedom of political expression expanded, and Ukraine's GDP doubled between 2004 and 2008. Unfortunately, the nation had made little headway against corruption, and the power of the rich oligarchs bedeviled the country's political life.

Ukraine's struggle mirrored what transpired in many of the other post-Soviet states. Why was it taking so long for these countries to become more democratic? The Cold War had ended, and democracy had defeated communism, so what was the problem? Few in the West understood the complications of becoming an open society after decades of totalitarian rule.

❧

Growing frustration among Ukrainians, especially among the younger generation, erupted in 2013 as hundreds of thousands of citizens again gathered in Kyiv to protest. Their complaints echoed those of 2004: they wanted government reform and an end to corruption, and they wanted to become Europeans, no longer imperial subjects managed from Moscow. Unlike Russian students, who were labeled "Generation *Nyet* (No)" because of their reluctance to engage in politics, Ukrainian students played a significant role in the protests. Students numbered heavily among the "Heavenly Hundred" killed in Kyiv by government snipers.

Violent attacks against students in Independence Square (or, Maidan) brought more than half a million Kyivans to the downtown area to form a space of freedom—a sacred place in the country's history. The Kremlin-backed president fled, eventually escaping to Russia, and leaders of the opposition movement formed a new provisional government.

Just ten years after the Orange Revolution, Putin had failed once again to bring Ukraine under his control, and he was furious. We now know that after a brief conversation with a small number of his closest advisors on

February 22, 2014—note the date—Putin decided to bring Crimea back under Russian control. Four days later, armed men in green uniforms without any markings or identification took control of the Crimean parliament and installed a pro-Russian leader as the new prime minister. The Russian parliament then passed legislation to annex Crimea as an "act of historical justice." In the months that followed, paramilitary units trained by Russia, and eventually joined by Russian troops, moved into the Donbas region, home to a strong Russian minority.

Ukraine was ill-equipped to deter Putin's aggression in Crimea and in the self-proclaimed Donetsk and Luhansk people's republics. At this point in his presidency, Putin had decided to reassert Russia's power regardless of the West's response. Success in Crimea raised his approval ratings above 85 percent at home. Russians began viewing the outside world as an enemy, and a siege mentality pervaded the country.

Within Ukraine, this second revolution—aptly named the Revolution of Dignity—gave strong warning that Russia's actions must be countered, with or without support from the West. Ukrainians determined to build a well-trained and battle-ready army. The war begun in 2014 catalyzed a sense of unity among Ukrainians who sought a multilingual, multicultural state and an end to Russian intervention.

The memorial built in Kyiv honoring the Heavenly Hundred, who gave their lives fighting for freedom, galvanized Ukrainians. They wanted dignity and respect for their rich and diverse culture, and no autocrat in Moscow was going to take it away from them. For most citizens of Ukraine, the message was clear: no more Russian domination.

Civil society in Ukraine experienced a new burst of energy when thousands of Ukrainians, many of whom had participated in the Maidan protests, joined the Ukrainian army and various volunteer groups to fight Russia-backed separatists in the East. The desire for independence had grown and, by mid-2014, 90 percent of Ukraine's population shared this conviction. Down came 1,300 Lenin monuments and up went the drive to build a Ukrainian fighting force, less dependent on outside assistance.

On July 17, 2014, a Russian-made missile hit a Malaysian Airlines flight with 298 people on board, killing all passengers and crew. Since many of the passengers were Asian or European, this murder of innocent civilians by Russian-supported soldiers escalated into a global crisis. Western leaders began to support Ukraine and sanction Russian government officials and related businesses.

Cease-fire negotiations were conducted in September 2014 and February 2015, with German and French participation. The resulting documents, known as Minsk I and Minsk II, did little to resolve the conflict. Ukraine refused to accept any loss of territory or end its efforts to integrate with the West, and Putin's national security team showed no signs of ending their interventions in Ukraine.

The tenacious resistance of the Ukrainians and the growing support from their European neighbors set the stage for an agreement with the European Union that, among other things, created a free trade zone in Ukraine. Exports to Russia from Ukraine plummeted even as trade with European countries almost doubled. Visa-free travel to the EU also allowed millions of Ukrainians to visit Europe.

The two revolutions, in 2004–2005 and 2013–2014, convinced Western democracies that Ukrainians needed their partnership and that Russia's aggression and violations of international law had to be stopped. US and NATO countries offered military assistance and American and Canadian officers began to train Ukrainian officers. These close relationships would prove vital after February 2022.

In the presidential election in the spring of 2019, the country was struggling to defend itself from Russian attacks while trying to reform its political system. With a quarter of the population living at or below the subsistence level, plus corruption scandals plaguing Ukraine's leadership, the population protested by electing a political outsider: a comedian with a law degree. At the age of forty-one, Volodymyr Zelensky became the youngest president in the country's history and its first Jewish president.

An exceptional communicator, Zelensky speaks from the heart, delivering passionate messages to the average citizen. From the beginning of the Russian invasion on February 24, 2022, his message was clear: We will win this war. He also changed his dress code, replacing the traditional coat and tie with the dark green T-shirt and M-Tac jacket of a Ukrainian volunteer. He wore the same outfit even when speaking to the US Congress and the British Parliament. It was a powerful symbol to his people: I am an ordinary citizen, an anti-tsar. The contrast with Putin could not be greater.

Ukraine has one more asset. Unlike Russia, its government and religious leaders have supported religious freedom. I have witnessed firsthand an ecumenical climate that welcomes all religions and even encourages shared religious services. Christian schools and nonprofit organizations began to flourish and reach out to the vulnerable in their society. Recognizing this climate, the UN has relied heavily on religious organizations as trust-worthy distribution centers for humanitarian aid.

Ukraine is an independent, sovereign state with a rich history and culture. Those who fight against their aggressors want to preserve the multicultural, multilanguage heritage that reflects their national identity. Ukrainians know who they are and what they cherish. They also know that a defeat of Russia will bring an end to its colonial empire. It would mean "Europe whole and free," a goal expressed in 1989 when the Berlin Wall cracked apart. There is much at stake in this war, for the defense of democ-racies in Europe and around the world.

The Future for Ukraine and Russia

WHEN PHILIP AND I discussed the possible contents of this book, we both knew it would be a challenge. We sought to understand how and why, after the collapse of the Soviet Union, Ukraine and Russia chose such different paths for their future. As the two largest of the fifteen republics in the USSR (Union of Soviet Socialist Republics) these countries would have a major impact on the course that other post-Soviet states would take.

After Russia invaded Ukraine on February 24, 2022, the challenge took on a new dimension. Now we had to write in the midst of a war with no sure outcome in sight. It is still difficult to know how the struggle will end or how it will reshape the two warring countries, not to mention Europe and the rest of the global community.

The October 1917 revolution, which overthrew the Romanov dynasty after 304 years of repressive rule, set loose a wave of violence. The Bolsheviks murdered Tsar Nicholas II and his family and fought a five-year civil war costing millions of lives. In a telling contrast, the radical changes in Russia around 1991—including a ban on the Communist Party—provoked no violent protest. Few Russians defended the communist regime that had controlled the country for seven decades.

As those of us in the Christian Bridge delegation witnessed in 1991, government officials and leading intellectuals, faced with the possible disintegration of the Soviet empire, were looking for a moral and spiritual renewal in their nation. While Mikhail Gorbachev's dramatic reforms made him a hero in the West, his domestic policies roused opposition inside Russia. Boris Yeltsin, president of the Russian Republic, won the power struggle with Gorbachev and forced him to resign a few months later.

Russia slid toward a kind of imitation democracy, with no serious effort to balance power among the various branches of government or to nurture a political system with new parties and an engaged citizenry. By the end of 1993, barely two years after the collapse of the Soviet system, Yeltsin and his team ended Russia's brief flirtation with parliamentary democracy by attacking the Russian White House where the parliaments' leaders worked. He then revised the Russian constitution to bolster the presidential role. Democracy did not survive Yeltsin's presidency.

With some detours along the way, Ukraine moved in a very different direction, especially after the Orange Revolution of 2004 and the Revolution of Dignity in 2013–2014. Ukraine chose a clear path to democracy, with free elections, accountability for its leaders, freedom of speech and religion, and decentralized political power.

When Vladimir Putin came to power in Russia in 2000, he immediately began to assume control over independent news sources and convert them into propaganda outlets for the Kremlin. Viewing developments in Ukraine as a threat to his government's stability, he began to intervene repeatedly in the political life of his southern neighbor.

Russia's invasion of Ukraine in 2022 was not a new war. Rather, it ramped up an ongoing war begun in 2013–2014, when the Russians forcibly annexed Crimea. Their aggression soon spread to the Donbas, where Russia brazenly seized several Ukrainian regions. Over the next eight years, more than 14,000 Ukrainians died in conflict with Russian forces.

In late 2023, as I am writing, war grinds on with no end in sight, even as another war rages between Israel and Hamas. Naturally we want to know answers to such questions as how long the fighting will last, who will win, and whether Putin or Zelensky will survive the war. I have no answers to these questions and, when asked, I usually respond, "It's complicated" and "I am not a prophet." Nevertheless, I can sketch out a series of scenarios and track developments that suggest the possible futures of Russia and Ukraine.

UKRAINE'S FUTURE

To achieve their primary goal of pushing Russian forces out of the country, Ukrainian forces must continue to rely on NATO's sophisticated weapons systems, ammunition, and training. The Western alliance, led by the US and NATO and bolstered by generous financial support from members of the European Union, is vital to Ukraine's success.

If foreign aid starts to diminish—as European nations get distracted by other threats and by waning popular support, and if the United States begins to shift its focus to China and the Middle East, or becomes distracted by elections and domestic issues—then the pressure on Ukraine to negotiate with Russia will mount. Regardless, it seems evident that the Ukrainians will not stop fighting until they have driven out the Russian invaders. After absorbing the wanton destruction of their cities, and a succession of gruesome war crimes and genocidal acts, Ukraine has a definite mission: we want our freedom, and we will fight to the death to evict foreign forces. Partisan warfare by Ukrainians could continue for years.

Astute observers will be watching the prospect of NATO membership for Ukraine, a move that Vladimir Putin fiercely opposes. Membership requires the unanimous consent of all thirty-one members, and if membership in NATO is denied or indefinitely postponed, will that weaken support for Ukraine? Will converting Ukraine into a "porcupine state" like Israel—strong enough militarily to deter aggressors—become an option?

Ukraine faces enormous problems, including the immense task of rebuilding the infrastructure of the country. How will they care for the well-being of so many Ukrainian refugees and soldiers who must cope with trauma, broken families, and the reality of destroyed homes, farms, and businesses? Plus, who will pay for the reconstruction? Can the Russian government and its wealthy elites be held responsible for the damage that has been inflicted on their southern neighbor?

Just as important, if Ukraine recaptures territory under Russian occupation, how can they counter the impact of ten years' worth of Russian media proclaiming a false narrative about their country? Putin refers to those regions as Novorossiya, or New Russia. Can Ukraine recapture the hearts and minds of its citizens who have been living under Russian control for a decade? Thousands of men in the Russian-occupied regions have been conscripted to fight against Ukraine, and many have died. As President Zelensky himself dryly admits, "We need to be ready for the fact that some of those people will not be happy to see us."

Harvard professor Serhii Plokhy argues that the Russian-Ukrainian war is "the first 'good war' since the global conflict of 1939–1945, in which it was very clear from the start who was the aggressor and who the victim, who was the villain and who the hero, and whose side one wanted to be on." Because Ukraine has bravely resisted the Russian assault and received support from a large alliance of other nations led by the US and NATO, Plokhy and other analysts remain convinced that Ukraine has ensured its future as an independent state and nation. This war for survival has made Ukraine more united and more certain of its identity than ever before.

President Zelensky's former press secretary, Iuliia Mendel, describes the Ukrainians' new spirit in her book *The Fight of Our Lives*: "Out of all this pain [of the war], there is one thing I do know: this war, like the fiery breath of an enraged dragon, has burned away all that was artificial and superficial in our lives. . . . We have seen the immense power that we derive from learning to work together as a people and a nation. . . . We Ukrainians will never give up—not to Russia, not to terror or any other evil. . . . I have always believed in Ukraine. And I always will."

RUSSIA'S FUTURE

If Russia loses the war and is forced to withdraw its forces from Ukraine, any one of a number of results could follow. Putin might be deposed or forcibly removed from power, though no one knows who would emerge as Russia's next leader. In the history of autocracies, 80 percent of toppled autocrats are succeeded by other like-minded autocrats. The list of possible successors suggests little softening in the Kremlin's hostility toward the West. While another member of the Kremlin's national security council may ascend to power, and may end Russia's war effort in Ukraine, a tenuous peace might be the best long-term result.

Several leading scholars believe that Russia's defeat will bring an end to the Russian empire, Europe's last colonial power. Some foresee the fracturing of Russia, with ethnic minorities fighting for independence in regions such as Chechnya, while other scholars expect eastern Siberia and other regions to seek independence. Few expect a defeated Russia to regain status as a major power. The autocracy Putin has created and his regime of terror would take years to dismantle. Russia may remain a pariah state for some time, one similar to North Korea or Iran. NATO and the European Union will insist on war crimes trials and reparations for rebuilding Ukraine, and the sanctions that restrain the Russian economy may stay in place unless the Western powers scale them back if Russia starts to pay Ukraine's repair bills.

Russia's ambitions do not reflect reality. By any measure, Russia is an empire in serious decline. Economically, its profits from petroleum disguise an underlying weakness: for all of its gas and oil revenue, Russia's total exports in 2021 did not equal Belgium's. Demographically, Russia is losing population, a trend that has been carefully tracked by Nicholas Eberstadt at the American Enterprise Institute. For the past thirty years, deaths in Russia have exceeded births by a cumulative 15.7 million. Eberstadt estimates that Russia's population will shrink by a quarter in one generation, and that does not count the million or so Russians who fled after the invasion of Ukraine. On mortality charts, Russia's record falls below twenty-three of the forty-six countries categorized as "least developed."

Despite being a well-educated country, Russia's knowledge economy, too, is largely dysfunctional. The number of patents registered by Russia, the ninth largest country in population, puts it on par with the US state of Alabama. Eberstadt's research exposes the gap between Putin's risky foreign policy, with its attempt to recreate the Soviet empire, and "the reality of a society and economy hollowed out by poor health and lack of economic competitiveness." According to its 2010 census, the Russian Federation includes more than two hundred ethnic groups; the ethnic Russian share of the population is declining while its Muslim population is growing. Putin's grand ambitions simply do not match Russia's current assets.

If Ukraine cannot force Russian invaders out of their country and the war turns into a "frozen conflict," Putin or his successor may be able to rebuild the military and its industrial base. Putin's strategy seems to anticipate that the West will reduce its support for Ukraine if the war drags on. This could encourage Russia to return to the offense in Ukraine and to attack or subvert other countries on its borders.

Zelensky and his advisors, supported by the vast majority of Ukrainian citizens, will not forsake their efforts to defeat Russia until its colonial aggression has ended, with an appropriate punishment meted out to the Putin autocracy. They rightly stress that Russia's attack on Ukraine is merely the first step in Putin's empire-building efforts; Putin needs aggressions in order to sustain his power base in Russia. Possible future targets include the three Baltic states (Lithuania, Estonia and Latvia), Poland, Moldova, and Georgia, among others.

One looming question involves Russia's nuclear capability and its leaders' periodic threats to deploy these weapons if their country is threatened. Putin uses this threat to deter his enemies, but most analysts do not see the use of nuclear weapons as a serious option for the Kremlin leadership. A nuclear weapon offers limited battlefield advantages and has been strongly opposed by Russia's few allies. NATO and the United States have also warned the Kremlin that the use of a nuclear weapon will result in a non-nuclear response that will decimate Russia's military capabilities. Nonetheless, Russia has recklessly fired upon nuclear power stations, risking a Chernobyl-like catastrophe.

The fear of losing control of Russia's nuclear assets, as well as the potential for civil war resulting from Russia's dismemberment, makes some Western leaders wary of dealing too harshly with Russia. But the real threat to peace centers on Russia's autocracy, whether led by Putin or his successors; they need war in order to suppress internal dissension and to protect their power and stolen assets. A defeat of Russia by Ukraine offers the best hope for change in Moscow.

GLOBAL CONSIDERATIONS

Since 2007 Putin has bluntly expressed his hatred of the West, principally the United States. His propaganda portrays the Russia vs. Ukraine war as a Russia vs. US-and-NATO war. Arguing that Ukraine is a puppet of the West, he paints Russia as the victim, not the aggressor. He assumed the West was weak, that NATO had no backbone, and that the United States lacked the will to fight. He was wrong on all counts, and Ukraine and its allies rose to the challenge of opposing Putin's empire-building effort.

If Putin ultimately succeeds, other autocrats may well resort to aggression against their neighbors, especially if they possess nuclear weapons. On the other hand, if Putin loses, other dictators will note the consequences of aggression: a united military response from democratic countries and painful economic sanctions.

By attacking Ukraine, Putin hoped to undermine the international security system in Europe established after World War II, replacing it with a coalition led by Russia and its autocratic allies. He envisioned a multipolar world led primarily by Russia and China, and no longer by Western democracies. Instead, his miscalculations led to the re-emergence of the United States as the global leader of democratic nations. Putin saw US leadership reinvigorate NATO and unify the supporters of Ukraine. To Putin's dismay, the Russian-Ukrainian war recreated a bipolar Cold War, this time built on leadership from Washington and Beijing. To that degree, Putin has already "lost" the war in Ukraine.

Project Christian Bridge

The following was Project Christian Bridge's response to the Supreme Soviet's plea for help from Christian leaders in the United States:

The individuals of Project Christian Bridge come from a variety of Christian organizations. Our delegation includes educators, religious leaders, broadcasters, missionaries, scholars, and social workers. We are not coming to promote Americanism or capitalism, though we appreciate our country and are aware of the benefits free markets have provided. In fact, we are profoundly aware of our national shortcomings and are fearful that our national religious heritage is being undermined. The message of Project Christian Bridge transcends national loyalty and political and economic views. We unashamedly advocate Christian understandings of reality—understandings which transcend the differences between individuals of different religious persuasions.

Our purpose for coming is as follows:

1. To encourage understanding and facilitate cooperation between American Christians and the governments of the USSR, Russia, and Ukraine;

2. To promote Christian ideas and values as a means of positively influencing family life, social problems (alcoholism, crime, etc.), business ethics, education, democratic structures, humanitarian ventures, and charitable activities;

3. To support understanding and cooperation between Protestants, Orthodox, and Catholics;

4. To promote religious freedom and equality of rights for all religious groups.

We come in a spirit of friendship, committed to exploring ways we may assist the people of the USSR, Russia, and Ukraine in this time of pivotal transition in your society. Our desire to help springs from our Christian conviction that "faith without works is dead." Hence, we desire not only to share our beliefs, but also to demonstrate our concern by stimulating the Christian community to carry out acts of compassion. We are impressed with the openness in your society to discuss anew matters of ultimate significance such as man's relationship to God and the meaning and purposes of human existence.

We firmly believe that religious faith, particularly Christianity, is a source of meaning and values. Orthodox, Catholics and Protestants ought to work together to encourage the spread of basic Christian understanding. We believe Christian faith promotes patience, forgiveness, and compassion, as well as honesty and diligence. Though we advance our views with conviction, we insist on freedom for those who do not share our religious ideas. Further, we believe it is possible to cooperate with nonbelievers on the basis of natural law and cooperation with all people of good will.

We come in friendship to learn and to serve, to receive and to give. It is our prayer that Project Christian Bridge will unite us in the pursuit of noble goals.

Subject Index

Academy of Social Sciences, 60–65
aggressions, Putin needing, 148, 169
Aker, John, 21–22, 29
Andropov, Yuri, 3
anomie, 138, 139
Applebaum, Anne, 108, 144, 145
assassinations, under Putin's supervision, 89
atheism, 20, 64, 133, 154, 155, 156
atrocities, 118, 141, 160
August coup, 52, 55
autocracy, 144–52, 170
autocrats, 107, 144, 146, 168
awakening, signs of (photo), 74

Babi Yar, 100
Baltic states, 151–52, 169
Basil, 33–35, 38, 70, 72
Berlin Wall, fall of, 133
Bernbaum, John, 79
Bibles, distribution of, 21
Biden, Joe, 149
Bolsheviks, 153, 165
Brother Bonifato, 41, 43, 44, 46
Brezhnev, Leonid, 3, 50
"Brezhnev Doctrine," repudiation of, 5
Bucha, 114, 115, 116, 118, 126
Bulgakov, Mikhail, 133–34, 155
Bush, George H. W., 5, 21, 77
Bush, George W., 87, 93

Campus Crusade for Christ (CRU), 33, 82
capitalism, 59, 62, 83

"Christian America," US speeches about, 158
Christian Bridge. *See* Project Christian Bridge
Christian educators, delegation to the Soviet Union, 80
Christian liberal arts college, in Moscow, 79
Christian ministries, operating out of Irpin, 113
churches
    response of Ukrainian, 122
    Russian unprepared for societal changes, 156
Churchill, Winston, 35–36, 108
Cold War, 3, 5, 77, 78, 133, 170
CoMission, 82, 85
communism, vii, 12, 48, 131, 156
Communist Party
    ban on provoked no violent protest, 165
    leaders never apologized, 157
    model of a socialist society, 139
    monopoly on power, 5
    reaching out to evangelical Christianity, 55
    Russian Orthodox Church and, 39–40, 153
    in Ukraine, 100
    Yeltsin resigned from, 6
corruption, of Yeltsin's government, 96, 137
courage, as infectious, 108
Crimea, 103, 162
cultural genocide, 118–19, 141, 142

culture
    ignoring underlying, 131
    of Ukraine, 160
"culture war," 93

Declaration of Independence (U.S.),
    134
democracy
    battle between autocracy and, 144
    built on principles of human dignity,
       36
    converting a top-down system to,
       160
    as a dirty word, 85
    needing a culture of integrity, trust,
       and openness, 135, 137
    needing profound and systemic
       reform, 51
    Putin never had any intent to build,
       91
    Putin reversing, 96
    relationship with religion, 23
    in Ukraine, 100, 166
"denazifying," Ukraine, 120
Deyenka, Peter and Anita, 28, 74
dissent, Kremlin cracking down on, 89
Dmytruk, Natalia, 101
Dobson, James, 32
Dostoevsky, Fyodor, 43, 48, 58, 60, 64,
    67, 78, 155
double-talk, 95
Dzerzhinsky, Feliks, 25, 26

Eberstadt, Nicholas, 169
economic downturns, in Russia, 95
empires, Ukraine ruled by competing,
    141
energetic leadership, of Putin, 140
energy infrastructure, Russia's assault
    on, 118
energy sector, Putin's attack on
    Ukraine's, 149
energy superpower, Russia as, 149
ethnic groups, in Russian Federation,
    169
ethnic minorities, in Russia, 168
ethnic Russians, in Ukraine, 112
exodus of citizens, from Russia, 120

"failed states," allowing countries to
    become, 145
famine, in 1931–1933, 160
Famine Museum, in Kyiv, 99
foreign news sources, blocked by Rus-
    sia, 119
foreign policies, Gorbachev's shift in, 5
"forever war," Putin's attack on Ukraine,
    150
free market economy, 4, 160
freedom, 17–18, 62, 87, 147, 172
Freedom of Conscience Law, 20n1
"frozen conflict," 150, 169
FSB (Federal Security Service), 89

General Secretaries, of the Communist
    Party, 3, 4
genocide, on a massive scale, 118
glasnost (openness), 4, 49?
global politics, new threat in, 144
God, going where he is wanted, 70
"Godless shock brigades," 20
goodness, Russians lacking motivation
    for, 58
Gorbachev, Mikhail
    asked for help to restore morality, vii
    aura of fame of, 53
    coup against, 6
    domestic policies of, 165
    drawing comfort from the Bible, 51
    edged away from rigid Marxism,
       54–55
    granted full religious freedom, 52,
       154
    invited the Christian Bridge delega-
       tion, 13, 78
    meeting(s) with, 7, 14, 50, 52
    new era of change, 4
    new style of, 49
    orchestrating a revolution, 77
    photo, 73, 74
    presidential decrees, 20
    radical changes in the Soviet Union,
       80, 159
    reasons for his "new thinking,"
       131–32
    recognized contributions of Chris-
       tians, 155

rescue of, 27
resolve to end persecution of Christians, 5
on Russia's past failures, 154
Soviet cynicism about, 49
Gorbachev, Raisa, 14, 51, 60
Gorky Academic Choir, concert by, 81
Graham, Billy, visit to Moscow, 35
grief, breaking through, 125

health care facilities, Russian attacks on, 110
"Heavenly Hundred," memorials to, 102, 161, 162
Hill, Fiona, 86

imitation democracy, 159, 166
"Independence Generation," in Russia, 143
Independence Square (Maidan), 101, 102, 161
infrastructure (Ukrainian), 112, 167
Institute on Religion and Democracy (IRD), 63–65
Irpin, 113, 114
Irpin Bible Church, 122
Ivan, the agnostic, 64–65
Izium, war crimes in, 118
Izvestiya, 31, 55

"Jesus Film," in the Soviet Union, 82
Pope John Paul II, 40, 133
Joni and Friends, evacuated Ukrainians, 124
Journalists' Club of Moscow, visit to, 35–38

Kakhovka dam, demolished by Russians, 119
KGB (now FSB), 26, 28, 147
Kharkiv, Ukraine's surprise attack on, 111
Kherson, Russian humiliation in, 111
Khrushchev, Nikita, 3, 11, 50
Kiev. See also Kyiv
    as the mother of all Russian cities, 121
King, Martin Luther, Jr., 158

Patriarch Kirill, 92, 93, 94, 104, 121–22
knowledge economy, of Russia, 169
The Knowledge Society, 20
Kremlin, 24, 89, 94, 119, 155
Kyiv, 99, 106. See also Kiev

Law on Freedom of Conscience, 154–55
League of Militant Atheists, 20
Lenin, Vladimir, 48, 50, 57, 154
Leonovich, Alex, 21, 30–31, 34, 35, 72
life expectancy, for Russian males, 84
lines of people, at every storefront, 16
little green men, in Crimea, 103, 162
loyalists, chosen by Putin, 146
Lubenchenko, Konstantin, 21, 51, 71
Lubyanka prison, 26

Maidan Uprising. See Revolution of Dignity
Malaysian Airlines flight, downed by Russians, 162
Mariupol, destruction of, 117
Marx, Karl, 50, 57, 69
Marxism-Leninism, viii, 69, 132, 134, 144
Master and Margarita, The (Bulgakov), 133–34
material possessions, feverish pursuit of, 156
McFaul, Michael, 150
McIntire, Carl, 11, 12
media companies, autocrats buying, 144–45
Medvedev, Dmitry, 89
military and security forces, Putin's control of all, 148
ministry of presence, 124, 126
Minsk I and Minsk II, 163
Mission Eurasia, 113, 114
missionaries, 82, 85
mono-religious culture, of the Russian world, 157
moral foundation, seeking, 13, 82
moral life, rebuilding Soviet, 132
"moral revolution," in Russia, 135
morale, Ukrainian forces having a clear advantage of, 110

morality, 56, 132
Morgulis, Mikhail, 13, 21, 23
  on the existence of God, 52
  on the newscaster, 37
  photo, 71
  prayer in KGB meeting, 31
  response to Gorbachev, 51–52

national chaos, under Yeltsin, 96
national identity, confusion in Russia
  over, 139
national security establishment, enlarged by Putin, 147
nationalist movement, in Russia, 85
NATO, 106, 109, 149, 166–67
Navalny, Alexei, 89
Nederhood, Joel, 28, 51–52, 69–70
New Socialist Man, 57, 69
news sources, Putin's control over, 166
NGOs (Non-Governmental Organizations), 88
Tsar Nicholas I, 157
Nikkel, Ron, 35
  asking a prayer for the prisoners, 46
  on Basil, 33
  on cooperation with the Orthodox,
    40
  on Zagorsk prison, 43
Brother Nikodim, 43, 44
Nizhny Novgorod State University
  (NNSU), visit to, 80
Nobel Peace Prize, Gorbachev
  awarded, 49
Novorossiya (New Russia), 167
nuclear capability, of Russia, 169–70
nuclear weapons, Ukraine surrendered,
  100
Nunn, Sam, 133

Obama, Barak, 89
October 1917 revolution, 165
oligarchs (Russian), 84, 147–48
oligarchs (Ukrainian), 161
"On Combating Terrorism" law, 94
oppression, pattern of under Putin, 90
Orange Revolution, 101, 102–3, 161
Orthodoxy, as a cultural identification
  for Russians, 157

partnerstvo, with the United States, 6
perestroika, 4, 49, 78, 81, 132
perfect equality, of Soviet communism,
  16
persecution, of Christians, 156
"personalist autocracy," Putin's Russia
  as a, 145
personalist autocrats, replaced by autocratic successors, 150
Peter the Great, 136, 142, 153
Polanski, Dmitri, Russia's deputy ambassador to the UN, 105
police academy, bribing your way into,
  96
political opinions, Ukrainians expressing openly, 99
political prisoners, released by Gorbachev, 4
populism, of autocrats, 144
"porcupine state," converting Ukraine
  into, 167
power, preventing a transfer of, 145
Pravda, meeting with editors of, 54–59
prayer, with Gorbachev, 52
Presidential Prayer Breakfast, 21
Prigozhin, Yevgeny, 146
Prison Fellowship, possibility of, 45
private property, no such thing as, 68
privatized religion, not acceptable to
  Christians, 158
Project Christian Bridge, 12–13,
  171–72
  Gorbachev impressed with, 53
  report on, 77
  trip by, 137
"psychology of persecution," 156
Putin, Vladimir
  acknowledged the failure of com-
    munism, 140
  aligning with Orthodox Church's
    positions, 93, 157
  arresting protestors against the war,
    119–20, 147
  ascent of, 86–91
  attacks against Ukrainian infrastruc-
    ture, 112
  brought stability at a cost, viii

claiming baptism as a child, 93

as a demon from hell, 115

early life as a tough hoodlum, 86

intervening in Ukraine's political life,
160–61

invasion of Ukraine, 78, 143, 151

making decisions alone or with a
small group, 145

miscalculations in planning, 107

offering oligarchs financial help, 148

Orange Revolution and, 102–3

rebuilding a centralized Russian
state, 137, 146, 147

restoration of Orthodox churches, 92

resurrecting the policies of the Romanov tsars, 142

reviving the grand dream of a Russian world, 94–95

setting the rules of engagement in
Ukraine, 110

slammed shut the window for spiritual help, 79

sought to dismantle the international
order, 144

on Ukraine having no right to exist,
117

Rakhuba, Sergey, heading Mission
Eurasia, 113

Reagan, Ronald, 5

refugees, Europe opened its arms to
receive, 109

religion
freedom of, 64, 94, 155, 159, 163–64,
172

holding little interest for secular
scholars, 131

newfound interest in, 155

official in Russia, 157

as "the opium of the people," 154

resurgence of in the former USSR,
82

role in returning to elementary
moral values, 132

symbolism of, 154

religious communities, cooperation in
Russia, 97

religious faith, not dying out in the
Soviet Union, 133

repentance
of the KGB, 28

"suppression of the Russian spirit"
and, 135–36

Repentance (Tengiz Abuladze), 28, 134

repression, autocrats handling, 146

Revolution of Dignity, 102, 103, 140,
162

Romanov dynasty of Russia, 142, 153

Roosevelt, Franklin D., 108

ruble, free fall of, 17

Russia
accused Ukraine of staging the Bucha massacre, 115–16

ambitions not reflecting reality,
168–69

deep mood of dissatisfaction, 138

defeating militarily, 150

future of, 168–70

justification for the war, 120

as the largest country on earth, 81

seeking to control other countries in
the region, 151

Russian Armed Forces, cathedral of, 94

Russian bear, looking for something to
bite, 91

Russian Bible Society, reopening of, 52

Russian Civil War, massive loss of lives,
160

Russian empire, 118, 168

Russian Federation, illustrating Russia's
uniqueness, 139

Russian flag, replacing the red Soviet
flag, 49

Russian forces
attached Ukraine from three directions, 105

no strategic plan for occupying
Ukraine, 107

Russian leaders
campaign against God and religion,
20

seeing religion as a healing solution,
137

Russian leaders (*continued*)
on the true character of faith, 155

Russian Orthodox Church
  dissidents within welcomed openness, 93
  as dominant state-supported religion, 157
  giving a sense of stability and permanence, 43
  history of as blood-soaked ground, 159–60
  KGB's close relationship with, 29
  in the Lubyanka prison building, 47, 122
  making God approachable, 46
  on the Putin era a "miracle of God," 92
  Putin relying on support from, 92
  role of, 153
  as a substitute state ideology, 93
Russian parliament, passed legislation to annex Crimea, 103, 162
Russian speakers in Ukraine, protecting the rights of, 148
Russian White House, shelled by tanks, 84–85
Russian world, dream of, 94
Russian-American Christian University (RACU), 79, 95, 96–97
Russians
  anti-Ukraine under Putin, 140
  autocrats and, 160
  battling each other over power and money, 85
  blaming others for their troubles, 136
  fleeing to places like Turkey and Finland, 120
  as the largest ethnic minority in Ukraine, 99
  living in a very repressive environment, 147
  national reputation faded under Yeltsin, 83
  not feeling accepted in traditional churches, 156
  viewing the outside world as an enemy, 104
"Russia's soul," Yeltsin's public search for, 138–39

Russification, revived yet again under the Soviet Union, 142
Russkiy mir, elements of, 94

Sakharov, Andrei, 26, 27
Sasha, visiting the Zagorsk prison, 40–41
"Savior Gate," in the Kremlin wall, 24
scandals, plagued Yeltsin's administration, 84
secular state, USSR founded as, 154
security, layers of protecting Putin, 150
Sergey S., 113, 115
Father Sergy, preserved body of, 48
Shevardnadze, Eduard, 5
Snyder, Timothy, 160
Sochi Olympics, 90, 103
social engineering, as the wave of the future, 139–40
social justice, consistent implementation of, 132
Solzhenitsyn, Aleksandr, 12, 32, 39
  on absolute power of Soviet leaders, 48–49
  on Christianity, 82
  on the disasters that had befallen Russia? 69
  estimated sixty million Russians died at the hands of their own government, 153
  on "the gulag archipelago," 26
  as an honored citizen, 17–18
  reading Dostoyevsky, 65
  on repentance, 135–36
  as a source of spirituality, 155
  on Soviet communism, 78
  strip search of, 27
  on tyranny, 67
Soviet communists, invited Christian leaders from the United States, viii
Soviet Union. *See also* USSR
  chaos in, 19
  moved away from atheism, 32
  signs of awakening in, 67
  tried to be "good" without God, 58
"special military operation," 119
spiritual revival, not occurring in Russia, 156–57

spiritual values, Gorbachev on the need for, 132

Stalin, Joseph, 3, 49, 50, 134, 142, 153

state institutions, planting seeds of distrust in, 145

Stolyarov, Nikolai, 27–31, 137
    photo, 71

Sudden Russian Death Syndrome, 90

Supreme Soviet, meeting with, 19–24

teachers, Russian appealed for help, 82

tension, autocrats managing, 146

"This is Russia" phrase, 95

Tolstoy, Leo, 78, 155

train transport, free for refugees from Ukraine, 109

triumphalism, West responding with a spirit of, 83

Trotsky, Leon, 57

Trump, Donald, 90

tyranny, as a habit in Russia, 67

Ukraine
    David-vs.-Goliath stance of, 109
    deepening political and economic ties with the West, 104
    defending itself against an unprovoked Russian invasion, 151
    escape from the shackles of communism, 160
    fought fiercely for democracy, 131
    as free and democratic, 146
    future of, 166–68
    history and culture different from Russia's, 141
    invasion of as not a new war, 166
    meaning *borderland*, 141
    more Orthodox churches than Russia, 97
    provided weapons to civilians, 149
    Putin obsessed over, 140
    Putin ordered military action against, 103
    religious leaders of, 98
    spirit of independence and freedom, 143
    tilt toward Europe fed Russian paranoia, 103, 120

viewed as the "Bible Belt" in the Soviet Union, 97

Ukraine Evangelical Theological Seminary, 122–23

Ukraine Without Orphans (UWO), 123

Ukrainian Catholic University, 123

Ukrainian Evangelical Theological Society, 116

Ukrainian Orthodox Church, 97, 157–58

Ukrainians
    dynamic change after 2016, 143
    fierce streak of don't-tread-on-me independence, 99
    forcibly deported to Russia or Belarus, 119
    heroic resistance of, 149
    protecting the sovereignty of their country, 142–43
    valued freedom and individualism, 160

United States, 22, 134, 151, 167, 170

unity, sense of among Ukrainians, 162

"universal values" of the West, Putin rejecting, 90

"unvangelism" campaigns, stamping out all religious belief, 20

USSR, 7, 14, 77, 81. *See also* Soviet Union

Van Diest, John, photo, 74

Vladimir the Great, 42, 121

"Voice of America," news item about Christian Bridge on, 33

Volf, Miroslav, 126

war crimes, catalog of possible Russian, 118–19

wars of choice, 140, 148, 151

"We Shall Overcome," sang in English, 6

"Who are we?" core identity of Russia and Ukraine, 138, 143

Yahidne (north of Kyiv), war crime in, 116

Yancey, Philip, 74, 77, 134

Yashin, Ilya, 119

Yeltsin, Boris

attacked the Russian White House,
156, 166

banned Communist Party activities
from Russian soil, 68–69

called on the people to defend democracy, 6

content to let the Soviet Union
unravel, 81

cuts to government spending and
ending price controls, 83–84

finding a successor, 86

forced Gorbachev to resign, 163, 165

identified with the forces of democratic change, 6

invitation to Project Christian
Bridge, vii, 13

lost moral legitimacy, 85

meeting with, 7

no plan for building a new system of
governance, 83, 137

presidential decrees, 20

proposed a search for Russia's soul,
138–39

shut down *Pravda*, 55

started a war in Chechnya, 95

tried to dissolve parliament, 84

as a tyrant, 67

Yushchenko, Viktor, 100–101

Zagorsk Monastery, 40, 41–43, 73

Zagorsk Prison, 40, 43–46

Zelensky, Volodymyr, 108, 119, 120,
163

Printed in the USA
CPSIA information can be obtained
at www.ICGtesting.com
LVHW041157290824
789290LV00004B/20